CECIL RHODES
MAN AND EMPIRE-MAKER

Cecil Rhodes, Man And Empire-maker...

Catherine Radziwill (Princess)

Photo: E. H. Mills

THE RT. HON. CECIL J. RHODES

CECIL RHODES
MAN AND EMPIRE-MAKER

BY

PRINCESS CATHERINE RADZIWILL

(CATHERINE KOLB-DANVIN)

With Eight Photogravure Plates

NEW YORK
FUNK AND WAGNALLS COMPANY
1918

CONTENTS

LIST OF ILLUSTRATIONS

INTRODUCTION

THE recent death of Sir Starr Jameson reminded the public of the South African War, which was such an engrossing subject to the British public at the close of the 'nineties and the first years of the present century. Yet though it may seem quite out of date to reopen the question when so many more important matters occupy attention, the relationship between South Africa and England is no small matter. It has also had its influence on actual events, if only by proving to the world the talent which Great Britain has displayed in the administration of her vast Colonies and the tact with which British statesmen have contrived to convert their foes of the day before into friends, sincere, devoted and true.

No other country in the world could have achieved such a success as did England in the complicated and singularly difficult task of making itself popular among nations whose independence it had destroyed.

The secret of this wonderful performance lies principally in the care which England has exercised to secure the welfare of the annexed population, and to do nothing

Introduction

likely to keep them in remembrance of the subordinate position into which they had been reduced. England never crushes those whom it subdues. Its inbred talent for colonisation has invariably led it along the right path in regard to its colonial development. Even in cases where Britain made the weight of its rule rather heavy for the people whom it had conquered, there still developed among them a desire to remain federated to the British Empire, and also a conviction that union, though it might be unpleasant to their personal feelings and sympathies, was, after all, the best thing which could have happened to them in regard to their material interests.

Prosperity has invariably attended British rule wherever it has found scope to develop itself, and at the present hour British patriotism is far more demonstrative in India, Australia or South Africa than it is in England itself. The sentiments thus strongly expressed impart a certain zealotism to their feelings, which constitutes a strong link with the Mother Country. In any hour of national danger or calamity this trait provides her with the enthusiastic help of her children from across the seas.

The Englishman, generally quiet at home and even subdued in the presence of strangers, is exuberant in the Colonies; he likes to shout his patriotism upon every

Introduction

possible occasion, even when it would be better to refrain. It is an aggressive patriotism which sometimes is quite uncouth in its manifestations, but it is real patriotism, disinterested and devoid of any mercenary or personal motives.

It is impossible to know what England is if one has not had the opportunity of visiting her Dominions oversea. It is just as impossible to judge of Englishmen when one has only seen them at home amid the comforts of the easy and pleasant existence which one enjoys in Merrie England, and only there. It is not the country Squires, whose homes are such a definite feature of English life; nor the aristocratic members of the Peerage, with their influence and their wealth; nor even the political men who sit in St. Stephen's, who have spread abroad the fame and might and power of England. But it is these modest pioneers of "nations yet to be" who, in the wilds and deserts of South Africa, Australia and Asia, have demonstrated the realities of English civilisation and the English spirit of freedom.

In the hour of danger we have seen all these members of the great Mother Country rush to its help. The spectacle has been an inspiring one, and in the case of South Africa especially it has been unique, inasmuch as it has been predicted far and wide that the memory of the Boer War would never die out, and that loyalty

Introduction

to Great Britain would never be found in the vast
African veldt. Facts have belied this rash assertion,
and the world has seldom witnessed a more impressive
vindication of the triumph of true Imperialism than that
presented by Generals Botha and Smuts. As the leader
of a whole nation, General Botha defended its independence against aggression, yet became the faithful,
devoted servant and the true adherent of the people
whom he had fought a few years before, putting at their
disposal the weight of his powerful personality and the
strength of his influence over his partisans and country-
men.

CATHERINE RADZIWILL.

December, 1917.

CECIL RHODES

CHAPTER I

CECIL RHODES AND SIR ALFRED MILNER

THE conquest of South Africa is one of the most curious episodes in English history. Begun through purely mercenary motives, it yet acquired a character of grandeur which, as time went on, divested it of all sordid and unworthy suspicions. South Africa has certainly been the land of adventurers, and many of them found there either fame or disgrace, unheard-of riches or the most abject poverty, power or humiliation. At the same time the Colony has had amongst its rulers statesmen of unblemished reputation and high honour, administrators of rare integrity, and men who saw beyond the fleeting interests of the hour into the far more important vista of the future.

When President Kruger was at its head the Transvaal Republic would have crumbled under the intrigues of some of its own citizens. The lust for riches which followed upon the discovery of the goldfields had, too, a drastic effect. The Transvaal was bound to fall into the hands of someone, and to be that Someone fell to the lot of England. This was a kindly throw of Fate, because England alone could administer all the wealth

B
1

of the region without its becoming a danger, not only to the community at large, but also to the Transvaalers.

That this is so can be proved by the eloquence of facts rather than by words. It is sufficient to look upon what South Africa was twenty-five years ago, and upon what it has become since under the protection of British rule, to be convinced of the truth of my assertion. From a land of perennial unrest and perpetual strife it has been transformed into a prosperous and quiet colony, absorbed only in the thought of its economic and commercial progress. Its population, which twenty years ago was wasting its time and energy in useless wrangles, stands to-day united to the Mother Country and absorbed by the sole thought of how best to prove its devotion.

The Boer War has still some curious issues of which no notice has been taken by the public at large. One of the principal, perhaps indeed the most important of these, is that, though brought about by material ambitions of certain people, it ended by being fought against these very same people, and that its conclusion eliminated them from public life instead of adding to their influence and their power. The result is certainly a strange and an interesting one, but it is easily explained if one takes into account the fact that once England as *a* nation—and not as *the* nation to which belonged the handful of adventurers through whose intrigues the war was brought about—entered into the possession of the Transvaal and organised the long-talked-of Union of

Value of the Boer War

South Africa, the country started a normal existence free from the unhealthy symptoms which had hindered its progress. It became a useful member of the vast British Empire, as well as a prosperous country enjoying a good government, and launched itself upon a career it could never have entered upon but for the war. Destructive as it was, the Boer campaign was not a war of annihilation. On the contrary, without it it would have been impossible for the vast South African territories to become federated into a Union of its own and at the same time to take her place as a member of another Empire from which it derived its prosperity and its welfare. The grandeur of England and the soundness of its leaders has never come out in a more striking manner than in this conquest of South Africa —a blood-stained conquest which has become a love match.

During the concluding years of last century the possibility of union was seldom taken into consideration; few, indeed, were clever enough and wise enough to find out that it was bound to take place as a natural consequence of the South African War. The war cleared the air all over South Africa. It crushed and destroyed all the suspicious, unhealthy elements that had gathered around the gold mines of the Transvaal and the diamond fields of Cape Colony. It dispersed the coterie of adventurers who had hastened there with the intention of becoming rapidly rich at the expense of the inhabitants of the country. A few men had succeeded

3

in building for themselves fortunes beyond the dreams of avarice, whilst the majority contrived to live more or less well at the expense of those naïve enough to trust to them in financial matters until the day when the war arrived to put an end to their plunderings.

The struggle into which President Kruger was compelled to rush was expected by some of the powerful intriguers in South Africa to result in increasing the influence of certain of the millionaires, who up to the time when the war broke out had ruled the Transvaal and indirectly the Cape Colony by the strength and importance of their riches. Instead, it weakened and then destroyed their power. Without the war South Africa would have grown more wicked, and matters there were bound soon to come to a crisis of some sort. The crux of the situation was whether this crisis was going to be brought about by a few unscrupulous people for their own benefit, or was to arise in consequence of the clever and far-seeing policy of wise politicians.

Happily for England, and I shall even say happily for the world at large, such a politician was found in the person of the then Sir Alfred Milner, who worked unselfishly toward the grand aim his far-sighted Imperialism saw in the distance.

History will give Viscount Milner—as he is to-day— the place which is due to him. His is indeed a great figure; he was courageous enough, sincere enough, and brave enough to give an account of the difficulties of the task he had accepted. His experience of Colonial politics was principally founded on what he had seen and studied when in Egypt and in India, which was a questionable equipment in the entirely new areas he was called upon to administer when he landed in Table Bay. Used to Eastern shrewdness and Eastern duplicity, he had not had opportunity to fight against the unscrupulousness of men who were neither born nor brought up in the country, but who had grown to consider it as their own, and exploited its resources not only to the utmost, but also to the detriment of the principles of common honesty.

The reader must not take my words as signifying a sweeping condemnation of the European population of South Africa. On the contrary, there existed in that distant part of the world many men of great integrity, high principles and unsullied honour who would never, under any condition whatsoever, have lent themselves to mean or dishonest action; men who held up high their national flag, and who gave the natives a splendid example of all that an Englishman could do or perform when called upon to maintain the reputation of his Mother Country abroad.

Some of the early English settlers have left great remembrance of their useful activity in the matter of the colonisation of the new continent to which they had emigrated, and their descendants, of whom I am happy to say there are a great number, have not shown themselves in any way unworthy of their forbears. South Africa has its statesmen and politicians who, having been born there, understand perfectly well its necessities and its wants. Unfortunately, for a time their voices were crushed by the new-comers who had invaded the country, and who considered themselves better able than anyone else to administer its affairs. They brought along with them fresh, strange ambitions, unscrupulousness, determination to obtain power for the furtherance of their personal aims, and a greed which the circumstances in which they found themselves placed was bound to develop into something even worse than a vice, because it made light of human life as well as of human property.

In any judgment on South Africa one must never forget that, after all, before the war did the work of a scavenger it was nothing else but a vast mining camp, with all its terrifying moods, its abject defects, and its indifference with regard to morals and to means. The first men who began to exploit the riches of that vast territory contrived in a relatively easy way to build up their fortunes upon a solid basis, but many of their followers, eager to walk in their steps, found difficulties upon which they had not reckoned or even thought about. In order to put them aside they used whatever means lay in their power, without hesitation as to whether these answered to the principles of honesty and straightforwardness. Their ruthless conduct was so far advantageous to their future schemes that it inspired disgust among those whose ancestors had sought a prosperity founded on hard work and conscientious toil. These good folk retired from the field, leaving it free to the adventurers who were to give such a bad name to England and who boasted loudly that they had been given full powers to do what they liked in the way of conquering a continent which, but for them, would have been only too glad to place itself under English protection and English rule. To these people, and to these alone, were due all the antagonisms which at last brought about the Boer War.

It was with these people that Sir Alfred Milner found himself out of harmony; from the first moment that he had set his foot on African soil they tried to put difficulties in his way, after they had convinced themselves that he would never consent to lend himself to their schemes.

Lord Milner has never belonged to the class of men who allow themselves to be influenced either by wealth or by the social position of anyone. He is perhaps one of the best judges of humanity it has been my fortune to meet, and though by no means an unkind judge, yet a very fair one. Intrigue is repulsive to him, and unless I am very much mistaken I venture to affirm that, in the 'nineties, because of the intrigues in which they indulged, he grew to loathe some of the men with whom he was thrown into contact. Yet he could not help seeing that these reckless speculators controlled public opinion in South Africa, and his political instinct compelled him to avail himself of their help, as without them he would not have been able to arrive at a proper understanding of the entanglements and complications of South African politics.

Previous to Sir Alfred's appointment as Governor of the Cape of Good Hope the office had been filled by men who, though of undoubted integrity and high standing, were yet unable to gauge the volume of intrigue with which they had to cope from those who had already established an iron—or, rather, golden—rule in South Africa.

Coteries of men whose sole aim was the amassing of quick fortunes were virtual rulers of Cape Colony, with more power than the Government to whom they simulated submission. All sorts of weird stories were in circulation. One popular belief was that the mutiny of the Dutch in Cape Colony just before the Boer War was at bottom due to the influence of money. This was followed by a feeling that, but for the aggressive operations of the outpost agents of certain commercial magnates, it would have been possible for England to realise the Union of South Africa by peaceful means instead of the bloody arbitrament of war.

In the minds of many Dutchmen—and Dutchmen who were sincerely patriotic Transvaalers—the conviction was strong that the natural capabilities of Boers did not lie in the direction of developing, as they could be, the amazing wealth-producing resources of the Transvaal and of the Orange Free State. By British help alone, such men believed, could their country hope to thrive as it ought.

A Magic Name

Here, then, was the nucleus around which the peaceful union of Boer and English peoples in South Africa could be achieved without bloodshed. Indeed, had Queen Victoria been represented at the Cape by Sir Alfred Milner ten years before he was appointed Governor there, many things which had a disastrous influence on the Dutch elements in South Africa would not have occurred. The Jameson Raid would certainly not have been planned and attempted. To this incident can be ascribed much of the strife and unpleasantness which followed, by which was lost to the British Government the chance, then fast ripening, of bringing about without difficulty a reconciliation of Dutch and English all over South Africa. This reconciliation would have been achieved through Cecil Rhodes, and would have been a fitting crown to a great career.

At one time the most popular man from the Zambesi to Table Mountain, the name of Cecil Rhodes was surrounded by that magic of personal power without which it is hardly possible for any conqueror to obtain the material or moral successes that give him a place in history; that win for him the love, the respect, and sometimes the hatred, of his contemporaries. Sir Alfred Milner would have known how to make the work of Cecil Rhodes of permanent value to the British Empire. It was a thousand pities that when Sir Alfred Milner took office in South Africa the influence of Cecil Rhodes, at one time politically dominant, had so materially shrunk as a definitive political factor.

Cecil Rhodes

Sir Alfred Milner found himself in the presence of a position already compromised beyond redemption, and obliged to fight against evils which ought never to have been allowed to develop. Even at that time, however, it would have been possible for Sir Alfred Milner to find a way of disposing of the various difficulties connected with English rule in South Africa had he been properly seconded by Mr. Rhodes. Unfortunately for both of them, their antagonism to each other, in their conception of what ought or ought not to be done in political matters, was further aggravated by intrigues which tended to keep Rhodes apart from the Queen's High Commissioner in South Africa.

It would not at all have suited certain people had Sir Alfred contrived to acquire a definite influence over Mr. Rhodes, and assuredly this would have happened had the two men have been allowed unhindered to appreciate the mental standard of each other. Mr. Rhodes was at heart a sincere patriot, and it was sufficient to make an appeal to his feelings of attachment to his Mother Country to cause him to look at things from that point of view. Had there existed any real intimacy between Groote Schuur and Government House at Cape Town, the whole course of South African politics might have been very different.

Sir Alfred Milner arrived in Cape Town with a singularly free and unbiased mind, determined not to allow other people's opinions to influence his own, and also to use all the means at his disposal to uphold the authority of the Queen without entering into conflict with anyone. He had heard a deal about the enmity of English and Dutch, but though he perfectly well realised its cause he had made up his mind to examine the situation for himself. He was not one of those who thought that the raid alone was responsible; he knew very well that this lamentable affair had only fanned into an open blaze years-long smoulderings of discontent. The Raid had been a consequence, not an isolated spontaneous act. Little by little over a long span of years the ambitious and sordid overridings of various restless, and too often reckless, adventurers had come to be considered as representative of English rule, English opinions and, what was still more unfortunate, England's personality as an Empire and as a nation.

On the other side of the matter, the Dutch—who were inconceivably ignorant—thought their little domain the pivot of the world. Blind to realities, they had no idea of the legitimate relative comparison between the Transvaal and the British Empire, and so grew arrogantly oppressive in their attitude towards British settlers and the powers at Cape Town.

All this naturally tinctured native feeling. Suspicion was fostered among the tribes, guns and ammunition percolated through Boer channels, the blacks viewed with disdain the friendly advances made by the British, and the atmosphere was thick with mutual distrust. The knowledge that this was the situation could not but impress painfully a delicate and proud mind, and surely

Lord Milner can be forgiven for the illusion which he at one time undoubtedly cherished that he would be able to dispel this false notion about his Mother Country that pervaded South Africa.

The Governor had not the least animosity against the Dutch, and at first the Boers had no feeling that Sir Alfred was prejudiced against them. Such a thought was drilled into their minds by subtle and cunning people who, for their own avaricious ends, desired to estrange the High Commissioner from the Afrikanders. Sir Alfred was represented as a tyrannical, unscrupulous man, whose one aim in life was the destruction of every vestige of Dutch independence, Dutch self-government and Dutch influence in Africa. Those who thus maligned him applied themselves to make him unpopular and to render his task so very uncongenial and unpleasant for him that he would at last give it up of his own accord, or else become the object of such violent hatreds that the Home Government would feel compelled to recall him. Thus they would be rid of the presence of a personage possessed of a sufficient energy to oppose them, and they would no longer need to fear his observant eyes. Sir Alfred Milner saw himself surrounded by all sorts of difficulties, and every attempt he made to bring forward his own plans for the settlement of the South African question crumbled to the ground almost before he could begin to work at it. Small wonder, therefore, if he felt discouraged and began to form a false opinion concerning the persons or the facts with whom he had

12

to deal. Those who might have helped him were constrained, without it being his fault. Mr. Rhodes became persuaded that the new Governor of Cape Colony had arrived there with preconceived notions in regard to himself. He was led to believe that Milner's firm determination was to crush him; that, moreover, he was jealous of him and of the work he had done in South Africa.

Incredible as it appears, Rhodes believed this absurd fiction, and learned to look upon Sir Alfred Milner as a natural enemy, desirous of thwarting him at every step. The Bloemfontein Conference, at which the brilliant qualities and the conciliating spirit of the new Governor of Cape Colony were first made clearly manifest, was represented to Rhodes as a desire to present him before the eyes of the Dutch as a negligible quantity in South Africa. Rhodes was strangely susceptible and far too mindful of the opinions of people of absolutely no importance. He fell into the snare, and though he was careful to hide from the public his real feelings in regard to Sir Alfred Milner, yet it was impossible for anyone who knew him well not to perceive at once that he had made up his mind not to help the High Commissioner. There is such a thing as damning praise, and Rhodes poured a good deal of it on the head of Sir Alfred.

Fortunately, Sir Alfred was sufficiently conscious of the rectitude of his intentions and far too superior to feelings of petty spite. He never allowed himself to be troubled by these unpleasantnesses, but went on his way without giving his enemies the pleasure of noticing the measure of success which, unhappily, attended their campaign. He remained inflexible in his conduct, and, disdaining any justification, went on doing what he thought was right, and which was right, as events proved subsequently. Although Milner had at last to give up, yet it is very largely due to him that the South African Union was ultimately constituted, and that the much-talked-of reconciliation of the Dutch and English in Cape Colony and in the Transvaal became an accomplished fact. Had Sir Alfred been listened to from the very beginning it might have taken place sooner, and perhaps the Boer War altogether avoided.

It is a curious thing that England's colonising powers, which are so remarkable, took such a long time to work their way in South Africa. At least it would have been a curious thing if one did not remember that among the first white men who arrived there Englishmen were much in the minority. And of those Englishmen who were attracted by the enormous mineral wealth which the country contained, a good proportion were not of the best class of English colonists. Many a one who landed in Table Bay was an adventurer, drawn thither by the wish to make or retrieve his fortune. Few came, as did Rhodes, in search of health, and few, again, were drawn thither by the pure love of adventure. In Australia, or in New Zealand or other colonies, people arrived with the determination to begin a new life and to create for themselves new ties, new occupations, new duties, so as to leave to their children after them the result of their labours. In South Africa it was seldom that emigrants were animated by the desire to make their home in the solitudes of the vast and unexplored veldt. Those who got rich there, though they may have built for themselves splendid houses while they dwelt in the land, never looked upon South Africa as home, but aspired to spend their quickly gained millions in London and to forget all about Table Mountain or the shafts and factories of Johannesburg and Kimberley.

To such men as these England was a pretext but never a symbol. Their strange conception of patriotism jarred the most unpleasantly on the straightforward nature of Sir Alfred Milner, who had very quickly discerned the egotism that lay concealed beneath its cloak. He understood what patriotism meant, what love for one's own country signified. He had arrived in South Africa determined to spare neither his person nor his strength in her service, and the man who was repeatedly accused both by the Dutch and by the English party in the Colony of labouring under a misconception of its real political situation was the one who had from the very first appreciated it as it deserved, and had recognised its damning as well as its redeeming points.

Sir Alfred meant South Africa to become a member of the British Empire, to participate in its greatness, and to enjoy the benefits of its protection. He had absolutely no idea of exasperating the feelings of the

Dutch part of its population. He had the best intentions in regard to President Kruger himself, and there was one moment, just at the time of the Bloemfontein Conference, when a *modus vivendi* between President Kruger and the Court of St. James's might have been established, notwithstanding the difficult question of the Uitlanders. It was frustrated by none other than these very Uitlanders, who, fondly believing that a war with England would establish them as absolute masters in the Gold Fields, brought it about, little realising that thereby was to be accomplished the one thing which they dreaded—the firm, just and far-seeing rule of England over all South Africa.

In a certain sense the Boer War was fought just as much against financiers as against President Kruger. It put an end to the arrogance of both.

CHAPTER II

THE FOUNDATIONS OF FORTUNE

IT is impossible to speak of South Africa without awarding to Cecil Rhodes the tribute which unquestionably is due to his strong personality. Without him it is possible that the vast territory which became so thoroughly associated with his name and with his life would still be without political importance. Without him it is probable that both the Diamond Fields to which Kimberley owes its prosperity and the Gold Fields which have won for the Transvaal its renown would never have risen above the importance of those of Brazil or California or Klondyke.

It was Rhodes who first conceived the thought of turning all these riches into a political instrument and of using it to the advantage of his country—the England to which he remained so profoundly attached amid all the vicissitudes of his life, and to whose possessions he was so eager to add.

Cecil Rhodes was ambitious in a grand, strange manner which made a complete abstraction of his own personality under certain conditions, but which in other circumstances made him violent, brutal in manner, thereby procuring enemies without number and detractors without end. His nature was something akin to that of the Roman Emperors in its insensate desire to exercise unchallenged an unlimited power. Impatient of restraint, no matter in what shape it presented itself, he brooked no resistance to his schemes; his rage against contradiction, and his opposition to any independence of thought or action on the part of those who were around him, brought about a result of which he would have been the first to complain, had he suspected it—that of allowing him to execute all his fancies and of giving way to all his resentments. Herein lies the reason why so many of his schemes fell through. This unfortunate trait also thrust him very often into the hands of those who were clever enough to exploit it, and who, more often than proved good to Rhodes' renown, suggested to him their own schemes and encouraged him to appropriate them as his own. He had a very quick way of catching hold of any suggestions that tallied with his sympathies or echoed any of his secret thoughts or aspirations.

Yet withal Rhodes was a great soul, and had he only been left to himself, or made longer sojourns in England, had he understood English political life more clearly, had he had to grapple with the difficulties which confront public existence in his Mother Country, he would most certainly have done far greater things. He found matters far too easy for him at first, and the obstacles which he encountered very often proved either of a trivial or else of a removable nature—by fair means or methods less commendable. A mining camp is not a school of morality, and just as diamonds lose of their value in the estimation of those who continually handle them, as is the case in Kimberley, so integrity and honour come to be looked upon from a peculiar point of view according to the code of the majority.

Then again, it must not be forgotten that the first opponents of Cecil Rhodes were black men, of whom the European always has the conception that they are not his equals. It is likely that if, instead of Lobengula, he had found before him a European chief or monarch, Rhodes would have acted differently than history credits him to have done toward the dusky sovereign. It is impossible to judge of facts of which one has had no occasion to watch the developments, or which have taken place in lands where one has never been. Neither Fernando Cortez in Mexico nor Pizzaro Gonzalo in Peru proved themselves merciful toward the populations whose territory they conquered. The tragedy which sealed the fate of Matabeleland was neither a darker nor a more terrible one than those of which history speaks when relating to us the circumstances attending the discovery of America. Such events must be judged objectively and forgiven accordingly. When forming an opinion on the doings and achievements of Cecil Rhodes one must make allowance for all the temptations which were thrown in his way and remember that he was a man who, if ambitious, was not so in a personal sense, but in a large, lofty manner, and who, whilst appropriating to himself the good things which he thought he could grasp, was also eager to make others share the profit of his success.

Cecil Rhodes, in all save name, was monarch over a continent almost as vast as his own fancy and imagination. He was always dreaming, always lost in thoughts which were wandering far beyond his actual surroundings, carrying him into regions where the common spirit of mankind seldom travelled. He was born for far better things than those which he ultimately attained, but he did not belong to the century in which he lived; his ruthless passions of anger and arrogance were more fitted for an earlier and cruder era. Had he possessed any disinterested friends capable of rousing the better qualities that slumbered beneath his apparent cynicism and unscrupulousness, most undoubtedly he would have become the most remarkable individual in his generation. Unfortunately, he found himself surrounded by creatures absolutely inferior to himself, whose deficiencies he was the first to notice, whom he despised either for their insignificance or for their mental and moral failings, but to whose influence he nevertheless succumbed.

When Cecil Rhodes arrived at Kimberley he was a mere youth. He had come to South Africa in quest of health and because he had a brother already settled there, Herbert Rhodes, who was later on to meet with a terrible fate. Cecil, if one is to believe what one hears from those who knew him at the time, was a shy youth, of a retiring disposition, whom no one could ever have suspected would develop into the hardy, strong man he became in time. He was constantly sick, and more than once was on the point of falling a victim of the dreaded fever which prevails all over South Africa and then was far more virulent in its nature than it is to-day. Kimberley at that time was still a vast solitude, with here and there a few scattered huts of corrugated iron occupied by the handful of colonists. Water was rare: it is related, indeed, that the only way to get a wash was to use soda water.

The beginning of Rhodes' fortune, if we are to believe what we are told, was an ice machine which he started in partnership with another settler. The produce they sold to their companions at an exorbitant price, but not for long; whereafter the enterprising young man proceeded to buy some plots of ground, of whose prolificacy in diamonds he had good reason to be aware. It must be here remarked that Rhodes was never a poor man; he could indulge in experiments as to his manner of investing his capital. And he was not slow to take advantage of this circumstance. Kimberley was a wild place at that time, and its distance from the civilised world, as well as the fact that nothing was controlled by public opinion, helped some to amass vast fortunes and put the weaker into the absolute power of the most unscrupulous. It is to the honour of Rhodes that, however he might have been tempted, he never listened to the advice which was given to him to do what the others did, and to despoil the men whose property he might have desired to acquire. He never gave way to the excesses of his daily companions, nor accepted their methods of enriching themselves at top speed so as soon to be able to return home with their gains.

From the first moment that he set foot on African soil Rhodes succumbed to the strange charm the country offers for thinkers and dreamers. His naturally languid temperament found a source of untold satisfaction in watching the Southern Cross rise over the vast veldt where scarcely man's foot had trod, where the immensity of its space was equalled by its sublime, quiet grandeur. He liked to spend the night in the open air, gazing at the innumerable stars and listening to the voice of the desert, so full of attractions for those who have grown to discern somewhat of Nature's hidden joys and sorrows. South Africa became for him a second Motherland, and one which seemed to him to be more hospitable to his temperament than the land of his birth. In South Africa he felt he could find more satisfaction and more enjoyment than in England, whose conventionalities did not appeal to his rebellious, unsophisticated heart. He liked to roam about in an old coat and wideawake hat; to forget that civilisation existed; to banish from his mind all memory of cities where man must bow down to Mrs. Grundy and may not defy, unscathed, certain well-defined prejudices.

Yet Cecil Rhodes neither cared for convention nor custom. His motto was to do what he liked and not to trouble about the judgments of the crowd. He never, however, lived up to this last part of his profession

What Mr. Schreiner Discovered

because, as I have shown already, he was keenly sensitive to praise and to blame, and hurt to the heart whenever he thought himself misjudged or condemned. Most of his mistakes proceeded from this over-sensitiveness which, in a certain sense, hardened him, inasmuch as it made him vindictive against those from whom he did not get the approval for which he yearned. In common with many another, too, Cecil Rhodes had that turn of mind which harbours resentment against anyone who has scored a point against its possessor. After the Jameson Raid Rhodes never forgave Mr. Schreiner for having found out his deceit, and tried to be revenged.

Cecil Rhodes had little sympathy with other people's woes unless these found an echo in his own, and the callousness which he so often displayed was not entirely the affectation it was thought by his friends or even by his enemies. Great in so many things, there were circumstances when he could show himself unutterably small, and he seldom practised consistency. Frank by nature, he was an adept at dissimulation when he thought that his personal interest required it. But he could "face the music," however discordant, and, unfortunately for him as well as for his memory, it was often so.

The means by which Cecil Rhodes contrived to acquire so unique a position in South Africa would require volumes to relate. Wealth alone could not have done so, nor could it have assured for him the popularity which he gained, not only among the European colonists, but also among the coloured people, notwithstanding the ruthlessness which he displayed in regard to them. There were millionaires far richer than himself in Kimberley and in Johannesburg. Alfred Beit, to mention only one, could dispose of a much larger capital than Rhodes ever possessed, but this did not give him an influence that could be compared with that of his friend, and not even the Life Governorship of De Beers procured for him any other fame than that of being a fabulously rich man. Barney Barnato and Joel were also familiar figures in the circle of wealthy speculators who lived under the shade of Table Mountain; but none among these men, some of whom were also remarkable in their way, could effect a tenth or even a millionth part of what Rhodes succeeded in performing. His was the moving spirit, without whom these men could never have conceived, far less done, all that they did. It was the magic of Rhodes' name which created that formidable organisation called the De Beers Company; which annexed to the British Empire the vast territory known now by the name of Rhodesia; and which attracted to the gold fields of Johannesburg all those whom they were to enrich or to ruin. Without the association and glamour of Rhodes' name, too, this area could never have acquired the political importance it possessed in the few years which preceded, and covered, the Boer War. Rhodes' was the mind which, after bringing about the famous Amalgamation of the diamond mines around Kimberley, then conceived the idea of turning a private company into a political instrument of a power which would control public opinion and public life all over South Africa more effectually even than the Government. This organisation had its own agents and spies and kept up a wide system of secret service. Under the pretext of looking out for diamond thieves, these emissaries in reality made it their duty to report on the private opinions and doings of those whose personality inspired distrust or apprehension.

This organisation was more a dictatorship than anything else, and had about it something at once genial and Mephistophelian. The conquest of Rhodesia was nothing in comparison with the power attained by this combine, which arrogated to itself almost unchallenged the right to domineer over every white man and to subdue every coloured one in the whole of the vast South African Continent. Rhodesia, indeed, was only rendered possible through the power wielded in Cape Colony to bring the great Northward adventure to a successfully definite issue.

In referring to Rhodesia, I am reminded of a curious fact which, so far as I am aware, has never been mentioned in any of the biographies of Mr. Rhodes, but which, on the contrary, has been carefully concealed from the public knowledge by his admirers and his satellites. The concession awarded by King Lobengula to Rhodes and to the few men who together with him took it upon themselves to add this piece of territory to the British Empire had, in reality, already been given by the dusky monarch—long before the ambitions of De Beers had taken that direction—to a Mr. Sonnenberg, a German Jew who had very quickly amassed a considerable fortune in various speculations. This Mr. Sonnenberg—who was subsequently to represent the Dutch party in the Cape Parliament, and who became one of the foremost members of the Afrikander Bond —during one of his journeys into the interior of the country from Basutoland, where he resided for some time, had taken the opportunity of a visit to Matabeleland to obtain a concession from the famous Lobengula. This covered the same ground and advantages which, later, were granted to Mr. Rhodes and his business associates.

Owing in some measure to negligence and partly through the impossibility of raising the enormous capital necessary to make anything profitable out of the concession, Mr. Sonnenberg had put the document into his drawer without troubling any more about it. Subsequently, when Matabeleland came into possession of the Chartered Company, Mr. Sonnenberg ventured to speak mildly of his own concession, and the matter was mentioned to Mr. Rhodes. The latter's reply was typical : " Tell the —— fool that if he was fool enough to lose this chance of making money he ought to take the consequences of it." And Mr. Sonnenberg had to content himself with this reply. Being a wise man in his generation he was clever enough to ignore the incident, and, realising the principle that might is stronger than right, he never again attempted to dispute the title of Cecil John Rhodes to the conquest which he had made, and, as I believe, pushed prudence to the extent of consigning his own concession to the flames. He knew but too well what his future prosperity would have been worth had he remembered the document.

CHAPTER III

A COMPLEX PERSONALITY

RHODESIA and its annexation was but the development of a vast scheme of conquest that had its start in the wonderful brain of the individual who by that time had become to be spoken of as the greatest man South Africa had ever known. Long before this Cecil Rhodes had entered political life as member of the Cape Parliament. He stood for the province of Barkly West, and his election, which was violently contested, made him master of this constituency for the whole of his political career. The entry into politics gave a decided aim to his ambitions and inspired him to a new activity, directing his wonderful organising faculties toward other than financial victories and instilling within him the desire to make for himself a name not solely associated with speculation, but one which would rank with those great Englishmen who had carried far and wide British renown and spread the fame of their Mother Country across the seas.

Rhodes' ambitions were not as unselfish as those of Clive, to mention only that one name. He thought far more of himself than of his native land in the hours when he meditated on all the advantages which he might obtain from a political career. He saw the way to become at last absolutely free to give shape to his dreams of conquest, and to hold under his sway the vast continent which he had insensibly come to consider as his private property. And by this I do not mean Rhodesia only—which he always spoke of as " My country "— but he also referred to Cape Colony in the same way. With one distinction, however, which was remarkable : he called it " My old country," thus expressing his conviction that the new one possessed all his affections. It is probable that, had time and opportunity been granted him to bring into execution his further plans, thereby to establish himself at Johannesburg and at Pretoria as firmly as he had done at Kimberley and Buluwayo, the latter townships would have come to occupy the same secondary importance in his thoughts as that which Cape Colony had assumed. Mr. Rhodes may have had a penchant for old clothes, but he certainly preferred new countries to ones already explored. To give Rhodes his due, he was not the money-grubbing man one would think, judging by his companions. He was constantly planning, constantly dreaming of wider areas to conquer and to civilise. The possession of gold was for him a means, not an aim ; he appreciated riches for the power they produced to do absolutely all that he wished, but not for the boast of having so many millions standing to his account at a bank. He meant to become a king in his way, and a king he unquestionably was for a time at least, until his own hand shattered his throne.

Cecil Rhodes

His first tenure of the Cape Premiership was most successful, and even during the second term his popularity went on growing until the fatal Jameson Raid— an act of folly which nothing can explain, nothing can excuse. Until it broke his political career, transforming him from the respected statesman whom every party in South Africa looked up to into a kind of broken idol never more to be trusted, Rhodes had enjoyed the complete confidence of the Dutch party. They fully believed he was the only man capable of effecting the Union which at that time was already considered to be indispensable to the prosperity of South Africa. Often he had stood up for their rights as the oldest settlers and inhabitants of the country. Even in the Transvaal, notwithstanding the authority wielded then by President Kruger, the populace would gladly have taken advantage of his services and of his experience to help them settle favourably their everlasting quarrels with the Uitlanders, as the English colonists were called.

Had Cecil Rhodes but had the patience to wait, and had he cared to enter into the details of a situation, the intricacies of which none knew better than he, it is probable that the annexation of the Transvaal to the British Empire would have taken place as a matter of course and the Boer War would never have broken out. Rhodes was not only popular among the Dutch, but also enjoyed their confidence, and it is no secret that he had courted them to the extent of exciting the suspicions of the ultra-English party, the Jingo elements of which had openly accused him of plotting with the Dutch against the authority of Queen Victoria and of wishing to get himself elected Life President of a Republic composed of the various South African States, included in which would be Cape Colony, and perhaps even Natal, in spite of the preponderance of the English element there.

That Rhodes might have achieved such a success is scarcely to be doubted, and personally I feel sure that there had been moments in his life when the idea of it had seriously occurred to him. At least I was led to think so in the course of a conversation which we had together on this subject a few weeks before the Boer War broke out. At that moment Rhodes knew that war was imminent, but it would be wrong to interpret that knowledge in the sense that he had ever thought of or planned rebellion against the Queen. Those who accused him of harbouring the idea either did not know him or else wished to harm him. Rhodes was essentially an Englishman, and set his own country above everything else in the world. Emphatically this is so; but it is equally true that his strange conceptions of morality in matters where politics came into question made him totally oblivious of the fact that he thought far more of his own self than of his native land in the plans which he conceived and formulated for the supremacy of England in South Africa. He was absolutely convinced that his election as Life President of a South African Republic would not be in any way detrimental to the interests of Great Britain; on the contrary, he assured himself it would make the latter far more powerful than it had ever been before in the land over which he would reign. By nature something of an Italian *condottieri*, he considered his native land as a stepping-stone to his own grandeur.

For a good many years he had chosen his best friends among Dutchmen of influence in the Cape Colony and in the Transvaal. He flattered, courted and praised them until he quite persuaded them that nowhere else would they find such a staunch supporter of their rights and of their claims. Men like Mr. Schreiner,[1] for instance, trusted him absolutely, and believed quite sincerely that in time he would be able to establish firm and friendly relations between the Cape Government and that of the Transvaal. Though the latter country had been, as it were, sequestrated by friends of Rhodes— much to their own profit—Mr. Schreiner felt convinced that the Colossus had never encouraged any plans which these people might have made against the independence of the Transvaal Republic. Rhodes had so completely fascinated him that even on the eve of the day when Jameson crossed the Border, Mr. Schreiner, when questioned by one of his friends about the rumours which had reached Cape Town concerning a projected invasion of the Transvaal by people connected with the Chartered Company, repudiated them with energy. Mr. Schreiner, indeed, declared that so long as Mr. Rhodes was Prime

[1] Now High Commissioner for the Union of South Africa.

32

Photo: Elliott & Fry

THE RT. HON. W. G. SCHREINER

Miss Olive Schreiner

Minister nothing of the kind could or would happen, as neither Jameson nor any of his lieutenants would dare to risk such an adventure without the sanction of their Chief, and that it was more to the latter's interest than to that of anyone else to preserve the independence of the Transvaal Republic.

Talking of Mr. Schreiner reminds me of his sister, the famous Olive Schreiner, the author of so many books which most certainly will long rank among the English classics. Olive Schreiner was once upon terms of great friendship with Mr. Rhodes, who extremely admired her great talents. She was an ardent Afrikander patriot, Dutch by sympathy and origin, gifted with singular intelligence and possessed of wide views, which strongly appealed to the soul and to the spirit of the man who at that time was considered as the greatest figure in South Africa.

It is not remarkable, therefore, that Rhodes should fall into the habit of confiding in Miss Schreiner, whom he found was " miles above " the people about him. He used to hold long conversations with her and to initiate her into many of his plans for the future, plans in which the interests and the welfare of the Cape Dutch, as well as the Transvaalers, used always to play the principal part. His friendship with her, however, was viewed with great displeasure by many who held watch around him. Circumstances—intentionally brought about, some maintain—conspired to cause a cooling of the friendship between the two most remarkable personalties in South

Cecil Rhodes

Africa. Later on, Miss Schreiner, who was an ardent patriot, having discovered what she termed and considered to be the duplicity of the man in whom she had so absolutely trusted, refused to meet Cecil Rhodes again. Her famous book, "Trooper Peter Halkett of Mashonaland," was the culminating point in their quarrel, and the break became complete.

This, however, was but an incident in a life in which the feminine element never had any great influence, perhaps because it was always kept in check by people anxious and eager not to allow it to occupy a place in the thoughts or in the existence of a man whom they had confiscated as their own property. There are people who, having risen from nothing to the heights of a social position, are able to shake off former associations: this was not the case with Rhodes, who, on the contrary, as he advanced in power and in influence, found himself every day more embarrassed by the men who had clung to him when he was a diamond digger, and who, through his financial acumen, had built up their fortunes. They surrounded him day and night, eliminating every person likely to interfere; slandering, ridiculing and calumniating them in turns, they at last left him nothing in place of his shattered faiths and lost ideals, until Rhodes became as isolated amidst his greatness and his millions as the veriest beggar in his hovel.

It was a sad sight to watch the ethical degradation of one of the most remarkable intelligences among the men of his generation; it was heartrending to see him

A Dissimulator

fall every day more and more into the power of unscrupulous people who did nothing else but exploit him
for their own benefit. South Africa has always been
the land of adventurers, and many a queer story could
be told. That of Cecil John Rhodes was, perhaps, the
most wonderful and the most tragic.

Whether he realised this retrogression himself it is
difficult to say. Sometimes one felt that such might
be the case, whilst at others it seemed as if he viewed
his own fate only as something absolutely wonderful
and bound to develop in the future even more pros-
perously than it had done in the past. There was always
about him something of the " tragediante, comediante "
applied to Napoleon by Pope Pius VII., and it is absolutely certain that he often feigned sentiments which
he did not feel, anger which he did not experience, and
pleasure that he did not have. He was a being of fits
and starts, moods and fancies, who liked to pose in such
a way as to give others an absolutely false idea of his
personality when he considered it useful to his interests
to do so. At times it was evident he experienced regret,
but it is doubtful whether he knew the meaning of re-
morse. The natives seldom occupied his thoughts, and if
he were reminded in later years that, after all, terrible
cruelties had been practised in Mashonaland or in Matabeleland, he used simply to shrug his shoulders and to
remark that it was impossible to make an omelette without breaking some eggs. It never occurred to him that
there might exist people who objected to the breaking of

35

Cecil Rhodes

a certain kind of eggs, and that humanity had a right to be considered even in conquest.

And, after all, was this annexation of the dominions of poor Lobengula a conquest? If one takes into account the strength of the people who attacked the savage king, and his own weakness, can one do else but regret that those who slaughtered Lobengula did not remember the rights of mercy in regard to a fallen foe? There are dark deeds connected with the attachment of Rhodesia to the British Empire, deeds which would never have been performed by a regular English Army, but which seemed quite natural to the band of enterprising fellows who had staked their fortunes on an expedition which it was their interest to represent as a most dangerous and difficult affair. I do not want to disparage them or their courage, but I cannot help questioning whether they ever had to withstand any serious attack of the enemy. I have been told perfectly sickening details concerning this conquest of the territory now known by the name of Rhodesia. The cruel manner in which, after having wrung from them a concession which virtually despoiled them of every right over their native land and after having goaded these people into exasperation, the people themselves were exterminated was terrible beyond words. For instance, there occurred the incident mentioned by Olive Schreiner in "Trooper Peter Halkett of Mashonaland," when over one hundred savages were suffocated alive in a cave where they sought a refuge.

A Complex Personality

Personally, I remain persuaded that these abominable deeds remained unknown to Mr. Rhodes and that he would not have tolerated them for one single instant. They were performed by people who were in possession of Rhodes' confidence, and who abused it by allowing the world to think that he encouraged such deeds. Later on it is likely that he became aware of the abuse that had been made of his name and of the manner in which it had been put forward as an excuse for inexcusable deeds, but he was far too indolent and far too indifferent to the blame of the world at these particular moments to disavow those who, after all, had helped him in his schemes of expansion, and who had ministered to his longing to have a kingdom to himself. Apart from this, he had a curious desire to brave public opinion and to do precisely the very things that it would have disapproved. He loved to humiliate those whom he had at one moment thought he might have occasion to fear. This explains the callousness with which he made the son of Lobengula one of his gardeners, and did not hesitate to ask him one day before strangers who were visiting Groote Schuur in what year he " had killed his father." The incident is absolutely true; it occurred in my own presence.

At times, such as that related in the paragraph above, Rhodes appeared a perfectly detestable and hateful creature, and yet he was never sincere whilst in such moods. A few moments later he would show himself under absolutely different colours and give proof of a

37

compassionate heart. Generous to a fault, he liked to be able to oblige his friends, or those who passed as such, while the charitable acts which he was constantly performing are too numerous to be remembered. He had a supreme contempt for money, but he spoiled the best sides of his strange, eccentric character by enjoying a display of its worst facets with a "cussedness" as amusing as it was sometimes unpleasant. Is it remarkable, then, that many people who only saw him in the disagreeable moods should judge him from an entirely false and misleading point of view?

Rhodes was a man for whom it was impossible to feel indifference; one either hated him or became fascinated by his curious and peculiar charm. This quality led many admirers to remain faithful to him even after disillusion had shattered their former friendship, and who, whilst refusing to speak to him any more, yet retained for him a deep affection which not even the conviction that it had been misplaced could alter. This is a remarkable and indisputable fact. After having rallied around him all that was honest in South Africa; after having been the petted child of all the old and influential ladies in Cape Town; after having been accepted as their leader by men like Mr. Schreiner and Mr. Hofmeyr, who, clever though they were, and convinced, as they must have been, of their personal influence on the Dutch party and the members of the Afrikander Bond, still preferred to subordinate their judgment to Rhodes'; after having enjoyed such unparalleled confidence,

A Strange Situation

Rhodes had come to be spurned and rejected politically, but had always kept his place in their hearts. Fate and his own faults separated him from these people of real weight and influence, and left him in the hands of those who pretended that they were attached to him, but who, in reality, cared only for the material advantages that their constant attendance upon him procured to them. They poisoned his mind, they separated him from all those who might have been useful to him, and they profited by the circumstance that the Raid had estranged him from his former friends to strengthen their own influence upon him, and to persuade him that those who had deplored the rash act were personal enemies, wishful for his downfall and disgrace.

CHAPTER IV

MRS. VAN KOOPMAN

AMONG those with whom Rhodes had been intimate from almost the first days of his establishment in Cape Town and his entrance into political life was a lady who, for something like half a century, had been enjoying an enviable position throughout almost the whole of South Africa. Mrs. van Koopman was a Dutchwoman of considerable means and of high character. She was clever, well read, and her quick intelligence allowed her to hold her own in discussion upon any subject against the most eminent men of her generation. She had never made a secret of her Dutch sympathies, nor of her desire to see her countrymen given equal rights with the English all over South Africa. She was on excellent terms with President Kruger, and with President Steyn, whose personality was a far more remarkable one than that of his old and crafty colleague.

The leading South African political men used to meet at Mrs. van Koopman's to discuss the current events of the day. It is related that she was one of the first to bring to the notice of her friends the complications that were bound to follow upon the discovery of the gold fields, and to implore them to define, without delay, the position of the foreign element which was

40

certain to move toward Johannesburg as soon as the news of the riches contained in that region became public property.

If the English Government had considered the matter at once the complications which arose as soon as companies began to be formed would have been less acute. The directors of these concerns imagined themselves to be entitled to displace local government, and took all executive power into their own hands. This would never have happened if firm governmental action had been promptly taken. The example of Kimberley ought to have opened the eyes of the Mother Country, and measures should have been taken to prevent the purely commercial domain of the gold fields from assuming such strident political activities, and little by little dominating not only the Transvaal Republic, but also the rest of South Africa.

Mrs. van Koopman had cherished a great affection for Rhodes. Her age—she was in the sixties—gave an almost maternal character to the tenderness with which she viewed him. He had made her his confidante, telling her all that he meant to do for the welfare of the land which she loved so dearly. She thought he looked upon South Africa with the same feelings of admiration as she did.

The strength of her belief led Mrs. van Koopman to interest all her friends in the career of the young Englishman, who appealed to her imagination as the embodiment of all that was great and good. Her enthusiasm

Cecil Rhodes

endowed him with many qualities that he did not possess, and magnified those which he really had. When he consulted her as to his future plans she entered closely into their details, discussed with him their chances of success, advised him and used all her influence, which was great, in winning him friends and adherents. She trusted him fully, and, on his part, whenever he returned to Cape Town after one of his yearly visits to Kimberley, or after a few months spent in the solitudes of Rhodesia, his first visit was always to the old and gentle lady, who welcomed him with open arms, words of affection, and sincere as well as devoted sympathy. She had always refused to listen to disparagement of her favourite, and would never allow any of the gruesome details connected with the annexation of Rhodesia to be recited in her presence.

In Mrs. van Koopman's eyes there was only a glorious side to the Rhodesian expedition, and she rejoiced in the renown which it was destined to bring to the man who had conceived and planned it. She fully believed that Rhodes meant to bring English civilisation, English laws, the English sense of independence and respect for individual freedom into that distant land. The fact that lucre lay at the bottom of the expedition never crossed her mind; even if it had she would have rejected the thought with scorn and contempt.

Although the attacks upon Cecil Rhodes increased day by day in intensity and in bitterness, Mrs. van Koopman never wavered in her allegiance. She attri-

42

buted them to jealousy and envy, and strenuously defended his name. Mrs. van Koopman, too, rejoiced at any new success of Rhodes as if it had been her own. She was the first to congratulate him when the dignity of a Privy Councillor was awarded to him. After the Matabele Rebellion, during which occurred one of the most famous episodes in the life of Rhodes, Mrs. van Koopman had been loud in her praises of the man whom she had been the first to guess would do great things.

The episode to which I refer, when he alone had had the courage to go unattended and unarmed to meet the savage chiefs assembled in the Matoppo Hills, had, by the way, done more than anything else to consolidate the position of the chairman of De Beers in South Africa.

During the first administration of Cape Colony by Mr. Rhodes, when his accession to the premiership had been viewed with a certain suspicion by the Dutch party, Mrs. van Koopman made tremendous efforts to induce them to have full confidence in her protégé. And the attempt succeeded, because even the shrewd Mr. Hofmeyr had at last succumbed to the constant entreaties which she had poured upon him. Thenceforward Mr. Hofmeyr became one of Mr. Rhodes' firm admirers and strong partisans. Under the able guidance of Mrs. van Koopman the relations between the Dutch party and their future enemy became so cordial that at last a singular construction was put upon both sides of the alliance by the opponents of both. The accusation, already referred to, was made against Rhodes that he wished to make for himself in South Africa a position of such independence and strength that even the authority of the Queen might find itself compromised by it. As has been pointed out, the supposition was devoid of truth, but it is quite certain that the then Premier of Cape Colony would not have objected had the suzerainty been placed in his hands by England and British rule in South Africa vested solely in his person.

During a brief interval in his political leadership Rhodes pursued his work in Rhodesia. In those days the famous British South Africa Company, which was to become known as the Chartered Company, was definitely constituted, and began its activity in the new territories which had come under its control. Ere long, though, the tide of events brought him again to the head of the Government. This time, however, though his appointment had been considered as a foregone conclusion, and though very few had opposed it, he no longer met the same sympathetic attention and cooperation which had characterised his first administration of public affairs. The Colony had begun to realise that Mr. Rhodes alone, and left free to do what he liked, or what he believed was right, was very different from Mr. Rhodes under the influence of the many so-called financiers and would-be politicians who surrounded him.

An atmosphere of favouritism and of flattery had

changed Rhodes, whom one would have thought far above such small things. Vague rumours, too, had begun to circulate concerning certain designs of the Chartered Company (one did not dare yet mention the name of its chief and chairman) on the Transvaal. Rhodes was directly questioned upon the subject by several of his friends, amongst others by Mr. Schreiner, to whom he energetically denied that such a thing had ever been planned. He added that Doctor Jameson, of whom the man in the street was already speaking as the man who was planning an aggression against the authority of President Kruger, was not even near the frontier of the neighbouring Republic. The mere idea of such a thing, Rhodes emphatically declared to Mr. Schreiner, was nothing but an ill-natured hallucination to create bad blood between the English and the Dutch. His tone seemed so sincere that Mr. Schreiner allowed himself to be convinced, and voluntarily assured his colleagues that he was convinced of the sincerity of the Prime Minister.

The only person who was really alarmed at the persistent rumours which circulated in Cape Town in regard to a possible attack in common accord with the leaders of the Reform movement in Johannesburg against the independence of the Transvaal Republic was Mrs. van Koopman. She knew Rhodes' character too well not to fear that he might have been induced to listen to the misguided advice of people trying to persuade him that the Rhodesian adventure was susceptible of being repeated on a larger and far more important scale, with as much impunity and as little danger as the other one had been. Alarmed beyond words by all that she was hearing, she determined to find out for herself the true state of things, and, trusting to her knowledge of Rhodes' character, she asked him to call upon her.

Rhodes came a few afternoons later, and Mrs. van Koopman closely questioned him on the subject, telling him of the tales which were being circulated not only in Cape Town, but also at Kimberley and Buluwayo and Johannesburg. Rhodes solemnly assured her that they were nothing but malicious gossip, and, taking her hands in his own, he repeated that all she had heard concerning the sinister designs he was supposed to be harbouring against the independence of the Transvaal had absolutely no foundation. To add force to his words, he continued that he respected her far too much to deceive her willingly, and that he would never have risked meeting her and talking with her upon such a subject had there been the slightest ground for the rumours which were disturbing the tranquillity of the inhabitants of Cape Town. When he left her Mrs. van Koopman felt quite reassured.

Next morning Mrs. van Koopman told her anxious friends that she had received such assurances from Rhodes that she could not disbelieve him, and that the best thing which they could do would be to contradict all statements on the subject of a raid on the Transvaal that might come

Mrs. van Koopman and the Raid

to their ears. This occurred on an after-Christmas evening of the year 1895.

When the decisive conversation which I have just related was taking place between Mrs. van Koopman and Cecil Rhodes, Doctor Jameson and his handful of eager adventurers had already entered Transvaal territory. The Raid had become an accomplished fact. It was soon realised that it was the most deplorable affair that could have occurred for the reputation of Cecil Rhodes and for his political future. The rebound, indeed, was immediate; his political career came to an end that day.

The person who was struck most painfully by this disgraceful and cryingly stupid adventure was Mrs. van Koopman. All her illusions—and she had nursed many concerning Rhodes—were destroyed at one blow. She never forgave him. All his attempts to bring about a reconciliation failed, and when later on he would fain have obtained her forgiveness, she absolutely refused all advances, and declared that she would never consent willingly to look upon his face or listen to his voice again. The proud old woman, whose ideals had been wrecked so cruelly, could not but feel a profound contempt for a man who had thus deliberately lied to her at the very time when she was appealing to his confidence. Her aristocratic instincts arose in indignation at the falsehoods which had been used to dupe her. She would not listen to any excuse, would not admit any extenuating circumstances; and perhaps because

47

she knew in the secret of her heart that she would never be able to resist the pleadings of the man who had thus deceived her, she absolutely refused to see him.

Rhodes never despaired of being restored to her favour, and would have given much to anyone able to induce her to relent in her judgment as to his conduct. Up to the last he made attempts to persuade her to reconsider her decision, but they all proved useless, and he died without having been able to win a forgiveness which he craved for many years.

I used to know Mrs. van Koopman well and to see her often. I admired her much, not only on account of her great talents and of her powerful intellect, but also for the great dignity which she displayed all through the Boer War, when, suspected of favouring the Dutch cause to the extent of holding communications with the rebels all over the Cape Colony, she never committed any indiscretion or gave cause for any direct action against her. For some time, by order of the military authorities, she was placed under police supervision, and her house was searched for papers and documents which, however, were not found—as might have been foreseen.

All through these trying months she never wavered in her attitude nor in her usual mode of life, except that she saw fewer people than formerly—not, as she used playfully to say, because she feared to be compromised, but because she did not wish to compromise others. More than once during my visits I spoke to her of Mr. Rhodes and tried to induce her to relent in her resolution. I even went so far as to tell her that her consent to meet him would, more than anything else, cause him to use all his influence, or what remained of it, in favour of a prompt settlement of the war in a peace honourable to both sides. Mrs. van Koopman smiled, but remained immovable. At last, seeing that I would not abandon the subject, she told me in tones which admitted of no discussion that she had far too much affection for Rhodes not to have been so entirely cut to the core by his duplicity in regard to her and by his whole conduct in that unfortunate matter of the Raid. She could trust him no longer, she told me, and, consequently, a meeting with him would only give her unutterable pain and revive memories that had better remain undisturbed. "Had I cared for him less I would not say so to you," she added, "but you must know that of all sad things the saddest is the destruction of idols one has built for oneself."

This attitude on the part of the one friend he had the greatest affection for was one of the many episodes which embittered Rhodes.

CHAPTER V

RHODES AND THE RAID

AFTER the Raid, faithful to his usual tactics of making others responsible for his own misdeeds, Cecil Rhodes grew to hate with ferocity all those whose silence and quiet disapproval reminded him of the fatal error into which he had been led. He was loud in his expressions of resentment against Mr. Schreiner and the other members of the Afrikander party who had not been able to conceal from him their indignation at his conduct on the memorable occasion which ruined his own political life. They had compelled him—one judged by his demeanour—to resign his office of Prime Minister at the very time when he was about to transform it into something far more important—to use it as the stepping-stone to future grandeurs of which he already dreamt, although he had so far refrained from speaking about them to others. Curious to say, however, he never blamed the authors of this political mistake, and never, in public at least, reproached Jameson for the disaster he had brought upon him.

What his secret thoughts were on this subject it is easy to guess. Circumstances used to occur now and then when a stray word spoken on impulse allowed one to discern that he deplored the moment of weakness into which he had been inveigled. For instance, during a dinner-party at Groote Schuur, when talking about the state of things prevailing in Johannesburg just before the war, he mentioned the names of five Reformers who, after the Raid, had been condemned to death by President Kruger, and added that he had paid their fine of twenty-five thousand pounds each. "Yes," he continued, with a certain grim accent of satire in his voice, " I paid £25,000 for each of these gentlemen." And when one of his guests tactlessly remarked, " But surely you need not have done so, Mr. Rhodes? It was tacitly admitting that you had been a party to their enterprise ! " he retorted immediately, " And if I choose to allow the world to think that such was the case, what business is it of yours? " I thought the man was going to drop under the table, so utterly flabbergasted did he look.

It is, of course, extremely difficult to know what was the actual part played by Rhodes in the Raid. He carried that secret to the grave, and it is not likely that his accomplices will ever reveal their own share in the responsibility for that wild adventure. My impression is that the idea of the Raid was started among the entourage of Rhodes and spoken of before him at length. He would listen in silence, as was his wont when he wished to establish the fact that he had nothing to do with a thing that had been submitted to him. Thus the Raid was tacitly encouraged by him, without his ever having pronounced himself either for or against it.

Cecil Rhodes

Rhodes was an extremely able politician, and a far-seeing one into the bargain. He would never have committed himself into an open approval of an attempt which he knew perfectly well involved the rights of nations. On the other hand, he would have welcomed any circumstance which would result in the overthrow of the Transvaal Republic by friends of his. His former successes, and especially the facility with which had been carried out the attachment of Rhodesia to the British Empire, had refracted his vision, and he refused —or failed—to see the difficulties which he might encounter if he wanted to proceed for the second time on an operation of the same kind.

On the other hand, he was worried by his friends to allow them to take decisive action, and was told that everyone in England would approve of his initiative in taking upon himself the responsibility of a step, out of which could only accrue solid advantage for the Mother Country.

Rhodes had been too long away from England, and his sojourns there during the ten years or so immediately preceding 1895 had been far too short for him to have been able to come to a proper appreciation of the importance of public opinion in Great Britain, or of those principles in matters of Government which no sound English politician will ever dare to put aside if he wishes to retain his hold. He failed to understand and to appreciate the narrow limit which must not be overstepped; he forgot that when one wants to perform

The Aim of the Raid

an act open to certain well-defined objections there must be a great aim in order eventually to explain and excuse the doing of it. The Raid had no such aim. No one made a mistake as to that point when passing judgment upon the Raid. The motives were too sordid, too mean, for anyone to do aught else but pass a sweeping condemnation upon the whole business.

If he did not, Rhodes ought to have known that the public would most certainly pass this verdict on so dark and shameful an adventure, one that harmed England's prestige in South Africa far more than ever did the Boer War. But though perhaps he realised beforehand that this would be the verdict, he only felt a vague apprehension, more as a fancy than from any real sense of impending danger. He had grown so used to see success attend his every step that his imagination refused to admit the possibility of defeat.

As for the people who engaged in the senseless adventure, their motives had none of the lofty ideals which influenced Rhodes himself. They simply wanted to obtain possession of the gold fields of the Transvaal and to oust the rightful owners. President Kruger represented an obstacle that had to be removed, and so they proceeded upon their mad quest without regard as to the possible consequences. Still less did they reflect that in his case they had not to deal with a native chief whose voice of protest had no chance to be heard, but with a very cute and determined man who had means at his disposal not only to defend himself, but also to appeal to European judgment to adjudge an unjustifiable aggression.

Apart from all these considerations, which ought to have been seriously taken into account by Doctor Jameson and his companions, the whole expedition was planned in a stupid, careless manner. No wonder that it immediately came to grief. It is probable that if Rhodes had entered into its details and allowed others to consult him, matters might have taken a different turn. But, as I have already shown, he preferred to be able to say at a given moment that he had known nothing about it. At least, this must have been what he meant to do. But events proved too strong for him. The fiasco was too complete for Rhodes to escape from its responsibilities, though it must be conceded that he never tried to do so once the storm burst. He faced the music bravely enough, perhaps because of the knowledge that no denial would be believed, perhaps also because all the instincts of his, after all, great nature caused him to come forward to take his share in the disgrace of the whole deplorable affair.

Whether he forgave Doctor Jameson for this act of folly remains a mystery. Personally I have always held that there must have *un cadavre entre eux*. No friendship could account for the strange relations which existed between these two men, one of whom had done so much to harm the other. At first it would have seemed as if an individual of the character of Cecil Rhodes would never have brought himself to forgive his confederate for the clumsiness with which he had handled a matter upon which the reputation of both of them depended, in the present as well as in the future. But far from abandoning the friend who had brought him into such trouble, he remained on the same terms of intimacy as before, with the difference, perhaps, that he saw even more of him than before the Raid. It seemed as if he wanted thus to affirm before the whole world his faith in the man through whom his whole political career had been wrecked.

The attitude of Rhodes toward Jameson was commented upon far and wide. The Dutch party in Cape Town saw in it a mere act of bravado into which they read an acknowledgment that, strong as was the Colossus, he was too weak to tell his accomplices to withdraw from public sight until the ever-increasing difficulties with the Transvaal—which became more and more acute after the Raid—had been settled in some way or other between President Kruger and the British Government. Instead of this Rhodes seemed to take a particular pleasure in parading the trust he declared he had in Doctor Jameson, and to consult him publicly upon almost all the political questions which were submitted to him for consideration. This did not mean that he followed the advice which he received, because, so far as I was able to observe, this was seldom the case.

To add to the contrariness of the situation, Rhodes always seemed more glad than anything else if he heard someone make an ill-natured remark about the Doctor,

Cecil Rhodes

or when anything particularly disagreeable occurred to the latter. An ironic smile used to light up Rhodes' face and a sarcastic chuckle be heard. But still, whenever one attempted to explain to him that the Raid had been an unforgivable piece of imprudence, or hazarded that Jameson had never been properly punished for it, Rhodes invariably took the part of this friend of his younger days, and would never acknowledge that Doctor Jim's desire to enter public life as a member of the Cape Parliament ought not to be gratified.

On his side, Doctor Jameson was determined that the opportunity to do so should be offered to him, and he used Rhodes' influence in order to obtain election. He knew very well that without it his candidature would have no chance.

Later on, when judging the events which preceded the last two years of Rhodes' life, many people expressed the opinion that Jameson, being a physician of unusual ability, was perfectly well aware that his friend was not destined to live to a very old age, and therefore wished to obtain from him while he could all the political support he required to establish his career as the statesman he fully believed he was. In fact, Doctor Jameson had made up his mind to outlive the odium of the Raid, and to become rehabilitated in public opinion to the extent of being allowed to take up the leadership of the party which had once owned Rhodes as its chief. By a strange freak of Providence, helped no doubt by an iron will and opportunities made the

56

most of, Jameson, who had been the great culprit in the mad adventure of the Raid, became the foremost man in Cape Colony for a brief period after the war, while Rhodes, who had been his victim, bore the full consequences of his weakness in having permitted himself to be persuaded to look through his fingers on the enterprise.

Rhodes never recovered any real political influence, was distrusted by English and Dutch alike, looked upon with caution by the Cape Government, and with suspicion even among his followers. The poor man had no friends worthy of the name, and those upon whom he relied the most were the first to betray his confidence. Unfortunately for himself, he had a profound contempt for humanity, and imagined himself capable of controlling all those whom he had elected to rule. He imagined he could turn and twist anyone according to his own impulses. In support of this assertion let me relate an incident in which I played a part.

When the Boer War showed symptoms of dragging on for a longer time than expected, some Englishmen proposed that Rhodes should be asked to stand again for Prime Minister, to do which he resolutely refused. Opinions, however, were very much divided. Some people declared that he was the only man capable of conciliating the Dutch and bringing the war to a happy issue. Others asserted that his again taking up the reins of Government would be considered by the Afrikander Bond—which was very powerful at the time

—as an unjustifiable provocation which would only further embitter those who had never forgiven Rhodes for the Raid.

A member of the Upper House of Legislature, whom I used to see often, and who was a strong partisan of Rhodes, determined to seek advice outside the House, and went to see an important political personage in Cape Town, one of those who frequented Groote Schuur and who posed as one of the strongest advocates of Rhodes again becoming the head of the Government presided over by Sir Alfred Milner. What was the surprise of my friend when, instead of finding a sympathising auditor, he heard him say that he considered that for the moment the return of Rhodes at the head of affairs would only complicate matters; that it was still too soon after the Raid; that his spirit of animosity in regard to certain people might not help to smooth matters at such a critical juncture; and that, moreover, Rhodes had grown very morose and tyrannical, and refused to brook any contradiction. Coming from a man who had no reason to be friendly with Rhodes, the remarks just reported would not have been important, but proceeding from a personage who was continually flattering Rhodes, they struck me as showing such considerable duplicity that I wrote warning Rhodes not to attach too much importance to the protestations of devotion to his person that the individual in question was perpetually pouring down upon him. The reply which I received was absolutely characteristic:

Rhodes' Personal Manner

"Thanks for your letter. Never mind what X——
says. He is a harmless donkey who can always make
himself useful when required to do so."

The foregoing incident is enlightening as to the real
nature of Cecil Rhodes. His great mistake was precisely in this conviction that he could order men at will,
and that men would never betray him or injure him
by their false interpretation of the directions which it
pleased him to give them. He considered himself so
entirely superior to the rest of mankind that it never
struck him that inferior beings could turn upon him and
rend him, or forget the obedience to his orders which
he expected them to observe. He did not appreciate
people with independence, though he admired them in
those rare moments when he would condescend to be
sincere with himself and with others; but he preferred
a great deal the miserable creatures who always said
"yes" to all his vagaries; who never dared to criticise
any of his instructions or to differ from any opinions
which he expressed. Sometimes he uttered these
opinions with a brutality that did him considerable
harm, inasmuch as it could not fail to cause repugnance
among any who listened to him, but were not sufficiently
acquainted with the peculiarities of his character to discern that he wanted simply to scare his audience, and
that he did not mean one single word of the ferocious
things he said in those moments when he happened to
be in a particularly perverse mood, and when it pleased
him to give a totally false impression of himself and

the nature of his convictions in political and public matters.

It must not be lost sight of when judging Mr. Rhodes that he had been living for the best part of his life among people with whom he could not have anything in common except the desire to make money in the shortest time possible. He was by nature a thinker, a philosopher, a reader, a man who belonged to the best class of students, those who understand that one's mind wants continually improving and that it is apt to rust when not kept active. His companions in those first years which followed upon his arrival in South Africa would certainly not have appreciated any of the books the reading of which constituted the solace of the young man who still preserved in his mind the traditions of Oxford. They were his inferiors in everything: intelligence, instruction, comprehension of those higher problems of the soul and of the mind which always interested him even in the most troubled and anxious moments of his life. He understood and realised that this was the fact, and this did not tend to inspire him with esteem or even with consideration for the people with whom he was compelled to live and work.

Men like Barney Barnato, to mention only this one name among the many, felt a kind of awe of Cecil Rhodes. This kind of thing, going on as it did for years, was bound to give Rhodes a wrong idea as to the faculty he had of bringing others to share his points of view, and he became so accustomed to be considered always right that he felt surprised and vexed whenever blind obedience was not given. Indeed, it so excited his displeasure that he would at once plunge into a course of conduct which he might never have adopted but for the fact that he had heard it condemned or criticised.

It has been said that every rich man is generally surrounded by parasites, and Cecil Rhodes was not spared this infliction. Only in his case these parasites did not apply their strength to attacks upon his purse; they exploited him for his influence, for the importance which it gave them to be considered by the world as his friends, or even his dependants. They appeared wherever he went, telling the general public that their presence had been requested by the " Boss " in such warm terms that they could not refuse. It was curious to watch this systematic chase which followed him everywhere, even to England. Sometimes this persistency on the part of persons whom he did not tolerate more than was absolutely necessary bored him and put him out of patience; but most of the time he accepted it as a necessary evil, and even felt flattered by it. He also liked to have perpetually around him individuals whom he could bully to his heart's content, who never resented an insult and never minded an insolence—and Rhodes was often insolent.

Another singular feature in a character as complex as it was interesting was the contempt in which he held all those who had risen under his very eyes, from comparative or absolute poverty, to the status of millionaires possessed of houses in Park Lane and shooting boxes in Scotland. He liked to relate all that he knew about them, and sometimes even to mention certain facts which the individuals themselves would probably have preferred to be consigned to oblivion. But—and here comes the singularity to which I have referred—Rhodes would not allow anyone else to speak of these things, and he always took the part of his so-called friends when outsiders hinted at dark episodes which did not admit of investigation. He almost gave a certificate of good conduct to people whom he might have been heard referring to a few hours before in a far more antagonistic spirit than that displayed by those whom he so sharply contradicted.

I remember one amusing instance of the idiosyncrasy referred to. There was in Johannesburg a man who, having arrived there with twenty-five pounds in his pockets—as he liked to relate with evident pride in the fact—had, in the course of two years, amassed together a fortune of two millions sterling. One day during dinner at Groote Schuur he enlarged upon the subject with such offensiveness that an English lady, newly arrived in South Africa and not yet experienced in the things which at the time were better left unsaid, was so annoyed at his persistency that she interrupted the speaker with the remark:

"Well, if I were you, I would not be so eager to let the world know that I had made two millions out of twenty-five pounds. It sounds exactly like the story of the man who says that in order to catch a train at six o'clock in the morning he gets up at ten minutes to six. You know at once that he cannot possibly have washed, whilst your story shows that you could not possibly have been honest."

I leave the reader to imagine the consternation produced among those present by these words. But what were their feelings when they heard Rhodes say in reply :

" Well, one does not always find water to wash in, and at Kimberley this happened oftener than one imagines; as for being honest, who cares for honesty nowadays? "

" Those who have not lived in South Africa, Mr. Rhodes," was the retort which silenced the Colossus.

This man of the get-rich-quick variety was one of those who had mastered the difficult operation of passing off to others the mines out of which he had already extracted most of the gold, an occupation which, in the early Johannesburg days, had been a favourite one with many of the inhabitants of this wonderful town. One must not forget that as soon as the fame of the gold fields of the Transvaal began to spread adventurers hastened there, together with a few honest pioneers, desirous of making a fortune out of the riches of a soil which, especially in prospectuses lavishly distributed on the London and Paris Stock Exchanges, was described as a modern Golconda. Concessions were bought and sold, companies were formed with a rapidity which savoured of the fabulous. Men made not only a living, but also large profits, by reselling plots of ground which they had bought but a few hours before, and one heard nothing but loud praises of this or that mine that could be had for a song, "owing to family circumstances" or other reasons which obliged their owner to part with it.

The individual who had boasted of the intelligent manner with which he had transformed his twenty-five pounds into two solid millions had, early in his career, invested some of his capital in one of these mines. Its only merit was its high-sounding name. He tried for some time without success to dispose of it. At last he happened to meet a Frenchman, newly arrived in Johannesburg, who wanted to acquire some mining property there with the view of forming a company. Our hero immediately offered his own. The Frenchman responded to the appeal, but expressed the desire to go down himself into the shaft to examine the property and get some ore in order to test it before the purchase was completed. The condition was agreed to with eagerness, and a few days later the victim and his executioner proceeded together to the mine. The Frenchman went down whilst Mr. X—— remained above. He walked about with his hands in his pockets, smoking cigarettes, the ashes of which he let fall with an apparent negligence into the baskets of ore which were being sent up by the Frenchman. When the latter came up, rather hot and dusty, the baskets were taken to Johannesburg and carefully examined: the ore was found to contain a considerable quantity of gold. The mine was bought, and not one scrap of gold was ever found in it. Mr. X—— had provided himself with cigarettes made for the purpose, which contained gold dust in lieu of tobacco, and the ashes which he had dropped were in reality the precious metal, the presence of which was to persuade the unfortunate Frenchman that he was buying a property of considerable value. He paid for it something like two hundred thousand pounds, whilst the fame of the man who had thus cleverly tricked him spread far and wide.

The most amusing part of the story consists in its *dénouement*. The duped Frenchman, though full of wrath, was, nevertheless, quite up to the game. He kept silence, but proceeded to form his company as if nothing had been the matter. When it was about to be constituted and registered, he asked Mr. X—— to become one of its directors, a demand that the latter could not very well refuse with decency. He therefore allowed his name to figure among those of the members of the board, and he used his best endeavours to push forward the shares of the concern of which he was pompously described on the prospectus as having been once the happy owner. As his name was one to conjure with the scrip went up to unheard-of prices, when both he and his supposed victim, the Frenchman, realised and retired from the venture, the richer by several hundreds of thousands of pounds. History does not say what became of the shareholders. As for Mr. X——, he now lives in Europe, and has still a reputation in South Africa.

This story is but one amongst hundreds, and it is little wonder that, surrounded as he was with men who indulged in this charming pastime of always trying to dupe their fellow creatures, Rhodes' moral sense relaxed. It is only surprising that he kept about him so much that was good and great, and that he did not succumb altogether to the contamination which affected everything and everybody around him. Happily for him he cherished his own ambitions, had his own dreams for companions, his absorption in the great work he had undertaken; these things were his salvation. Rhodesia became the principal field of Rhodes' activity, and the care with which he fostered its prosperity kept him too busy and interested to continue the quest for riches which had been his great, if not his principal, occupation during the first years of his stay in South Africa.

Although Cecil Rhodes was so happily placed that he had no need to bother over wealth, he was not so aloof to the glamour of politics. He had always felt the irk of his retirement after the Raid, and the hankering after a leading political position became more pronounced as the episode which shut the Parliamentary door behind him after he had passed through its portals faded in the mind of the people.

It was not surprising, therefore, to observe that politics once more took the upper hand amidst his preoccupations. It was, though, politics connected with the development of the country that bore his name more than with the welfare of the Cape Colony or of the Transvaal. It was only during the last two years of Rhodes' existence that his interest revived in the places connected with his first successes in life. Rhodes had been convinced that a war with the Boers would last only a matter of a few weeks—three months, as he prophesied when it broke out—and he was equally sure, though for what reason it is difficult to guess, that the war would restore him to his former position and power. The illusion lingered long enough to keep him in a state of excitement, during which, carried along by his natural enthusiasm, he indulged in several unconsidered steps, and when at last his hope was dispelled he accused everybody of being the cause of his disappointment. Never for a moment would he admit that he could have been mistaken, or that the war, which at a certain moment his intervention might possibly have avoided, had been the consequence of the mischievous act he had not prevented.

When the Bloemfontein Conference failed Rhodes was not altogether displeased. He had felt the affront of not being asked to attend; and, though his common sense told him that it would have been altogether out of the question for him to take part in it, as this would have been considered in the light of a personal insult by President Kruger, he would have liked to have been consulted by Sir Alfred Milner, as well as by the English

Government, as to the course to be adopted during its deliberations. He was fully persuaded in his own mind that Sir Alfred Milner, being still a new arrival in South Africa, had not been able to grasp its complicated problems, and so had not adopted the best means to baffle the intrigues of President Kruger and the diplomacy of his clever colleague, President Steyn. At every tale which reached Cecil Rhodes concerning the difficulties encountered by Sir Alfred, he declared that he was "glad to be out of this mess." Yet it was not difficult to see that he passionately regretted not being allowed to watch from a seat at the council table the vicissitudes of this last attempt by conference to smooth over difficulties arising from the recklessness displayed by people in arrogantly rushing matters that needed careful examination.

PRESIDENT KRUGER

CHAPTER VI

THE AFTERMATH OF THE RAID

TOWARD the close of the last chapter I referred to the Raid passing from the forefront of public memory. But though, as a fact, it became blurred in the mind of the people, as a factor in South African history its influence by no means diminished. Indeed, the aftermath of the Raid assumed far greater proportions as time went on. It influenced so entirely the further destinies of South Africa, and brought about such enmities and such bitterness along with it, that nothing short of a war could have washed away its impressions. Up to that fatal adventure the Jingo English elements, always viewed with distrust and dislike in the Transvaal as well as at the Cape, had been more or less held back in their desire to gain an ascendancy over the Dutch population, whilst the latter had accepted the Jingo as a necessary evil devoid of real importance, and only annoying from time to time.

After the Raid all the Jingoes who had hoped that its results would be to give them greater facilities of enrichment considered themselves personally aggrieved by its failure. They did just what Rhodes was always doing. The Boers and President Kruger had acted correctly in this enterprise of Doctor Jameson, but the

Cecil Rhodes

Jingoes made them responsible for the results of its failure. They went about giving expression to feelings of the most violent hatred against the Boers, and railed at their wickedness in daring to stand up in defence of rights which the British Government had solemnly recognised. It became quite useless to tell those misguided individuals that the Cabinet at Westminster had from the very first blamed Rhodes for his share in what the English Press, with but few exceptions, had declared to be an entirely disgraceful episode. They pretended that people in London knew nothing about the true state of affairs in South Africa or the necessities of the country; that the British Government had always shown deplorable weakness in regard to the treatment meted out to its subjects in the Colonies, and that both Rhodes and Jameson were heroes whose names deserved to be handed down to posterity for the services which they had rendered to their country.

It is true that these ardent Jingoes were but a small minority and that the right-minded elements among the English Colonials universally blamed the unwarranted attack that had been made against the independence of the Transvaal. But the truculent minority shouted loud enough to drown the censure, and as, with a few notable exceptions, the South African Press was under the influence of the magnates, it was not very easy to protest against the strange way in which the Raid was being excused. I am persuaded that, had the subject been allowed to drop, it would have died a natural death, or at worst been considered as an historical blunder. But the partisans of Rhodes, the friends of Jameson, and personages connected with the leading financial powers did their best to keep the remembrance of the expedition which wrecked the political life of Rhodes fresh before the public. The mere mention of it was soon sufficient to arouse a tempest of passions, especially among the Dutch party, and by and by the history of South Africa resolved itself into the Raid and its memories. You never heard people say, " This happened at such a time "; they merely declared, " This happened before, or after, the Raid." It became a landmark for the inhabitants of Cape Town and of the Transvaal, and I could almost believe that, in Kimberley at any rate, the very children in the schools were taught to date their knowledge of English history from the time of the Raid.

The enemies of Cecil Rhodes, and their number was legion, always declared that the reason why he had faced the music and braved public opinion in England lay in the fact that, for some reason or other, he was afraid of Doctor Jameson. I have referred already to this circumstance. Whilst refusing to admit such a possibility, yet I must own that the influence, and even the authority exercised by the Doctor on his chief, had something uncanny about it. My own opinion has always been that Rhodes' attitude arose principally from his conviction that Jameson was the only one who understood his constitution, the sole being capable of looking after his health. Curious as it may seem, I am sure the Colossus had an inordinate fear of death and of illness of any kind. He knew that his life was not a sound one, but he always rebelled against the idea that, like other mortals, he was subject to death. I feel persuaded that one of the reasons why he chose to be buried in the Matoppo Hills was that, in selecting this lonely spot, he felt that he would not often be called upon to see the place where he would rest one day.

This dread of the unknown, so rare in people of his calibre, remained with him until the end. It increased in acuteness as his health began to fail. Then, more than ever, did he entertain and plan new schemes, as if to persuade himself that he had unlimited time before him in which to execute them. His flatterers knew how to play upon his weakness, and they never failed to do so. Perhaps this foible explains the influence which Doctor Jameson undoubtedly exercised upon the mind of Rhodes. He believed himself to be in safety whenever Jameson was about him. And so in a certain sense he was, because, with all his faults, the Doctor had a real affection for the man to whom he had been bound by so many ties ever since the days when at Kimberley they had worked side by side, building their fortunes and their careers.

By a curious freak of destiny, when the tide of events connected with the war had given to the Progressive English party a clear majority in the Cape Parliament, Jameson assumed its leadership as a matter of course, largely because he was the political next-of-kin to

Hospitality at Groote Schuur

Rhodes. The fact that at that time he lived at Groote Schuur added to his popularity, and he continued whilst there the traditional hospitality displayed during the lifetime of Rhodes. That he ultimately became Prime Minister was not surprising; the office fell to his share as so many other good things had fallen before; and, having obtained this supreme triumph and enjoyed it for a time, he was tactful enough to retire at precisely the right moment.

The Raid indirectly killed Rhodes and directly obliterated his political reputation. It lost him, too, the respect of all the men who could have helped him to govern South Africa wisely and well. It deprived him of the experience and popularity of Mr. Schreiner, Mr. Merriman, Mr. Sauer and other members of the Afrikander Bond who had once been upon terms of intimacy and affection with him.

It must never be forgotten that at one period of his history Rhodes was considered to be the best friend of the Dutch party; and, secondly, that he had been the first to criticise the action of the British Government in regard to the Transvaal. At the very moment when the Raid was contemplated he was making the most solemn assurances to his friends—as they then believed themselves to be—that he would never tolerate any attack against the independence of the Boers. If his advice had been taken, Rhodes considered that the errors which culminated at Majuba with the defeat of the British troops would have been avoided. He caused the same assurances to be conveyed to President Kruger, and this duplicity, which in anyone less compromised than he was in regard to the Dutch party might have been blamed, was in his case considered as something akin to high treason, and roused against him sentiments not only of hatred, but also of disgust. When later on, at the time of the Boer War, Rhodes made attempts to ingratiate himself once more into the favour of the Dutch he failed to realise that while there are cases when animosity can give way before political necessity, it is quite impossible in private to shake hands with an individual whom one despises. And that such persons as Mrs. van Koopman or Mr. Schreiner, for instance, despised Rhodes there can be no doubt.

They were wrong in doing so. Rhodes was essentially a man of moods, and also an opportunist in his strange, blunt way. Had the Dutch rallied round him during the last war it is certain that he would have given himself up body and soul to the task of trying to smooth over the difficulties which gave such an obstinate character to the war. He would have induced the English Government to grant to all rebel colonists who returned to their allegiance a generous pardon and reinstatement into their former rights.

Even while the war lasted it is a fact that, in a certain sense, Rhodes' own party suspected him of betraying its interests. I feel almost sure that Sir Alfred Milner did not trust him, but, nevertheless, he would have liked Rhodes as a coadjutor. If the two men were never on sincerely cordial terms with one another it was not the fault of the High Commissioner, who, with that honesty of which he always and upon every occasion gave proof, tried to secure the co-operation of the great South African statesman in his difficult task. But Rhodes would not help Sir Alfred. But neither, too, would he help the Dutch unless they were willing to eat humble pie before him. In fact, it was this for which Rhodes had been waiting ever since the Raid. He wanted people to ask his forgiveness for the faults he himself had committed. He would have liked Sir Alfred Milner to beg of him as a favour to take the direction of public affairs, and he would have desired the whole of the Dutch party to come down *in corpore* to Groote Schuur, to implore him to become their leader and to fight not only for them but also for the rights of President Kruger, whom he professed to ridicule and despise, but to whom he had caused assurances of sympathy to be conveyed.

During the first period of the war, and especially during the siege, Cecil Rhodes was in Kimberley. He had gone with the secret hope that he might be able from that centre to retain a stronger hold on South African politics than could have been the case at Groote Schuur, in which region the only authority recognised by English and Dutch alike was that of Sir Alfred Milner. He waited for a sign telling him that his ambition was about to be realised in some way or other— and waited in vain.

Cecil Rhodes

It is indisputable that whilst he was shut up in the Diamond City Rhodes entered into secret negotiations with some of the Dutch leaders. This, though it might have been construed in the sense of treason against his own Motherland had it reached the knowledge of the extreme Jingo party, was in reality the sincere effort of a true patriot to put an end to a struggle which was threatening to destroy the prosperity of a country for which he had laboured for so many years.

In judging Rhodes one must not forget that though a leading personality in South Africa, and the chairman of a corporation which practically ruled the whole of the Cape Colony and, in part, also the Transvaal, he was, after all, at that time nothing but a private individual. He had the right to put his personal influence at the service of the State and of his country if he considered that by so doing he could bring to an end a war which threatened to bring destruction on a land that was just beginning to progress toward civilisation. It must be remembered that his was the only great personality in South Africa capable of opposing President Kruger and the other Dutch and Boer leaders. He was still popular among many people—feared by some, worshipped by others. He could rally round him many elements that would never coalesce with either Dutch or English unless he provided the impetus of his authority and approval. If only he had spoken frankly to the Boer leaders whom he had caused to be approached, called them to his side instead of having messages conveyed to them by people whom he could disavow later on and whom, in fact, he did disavow; and if, on the other hand, Rhodes had placed himself at the disposal of Sir Alfred Milner, and told him openly that he would try to see what he could do to help him, the tenseness of the situation would almost certainly have been eased.

In a position as intermediary between two adversaries who required his advice and influence to smooth the way toward a settlement of the terrible South African question Rhodes could have done incalculable service and added lustre to his name. But he did not, and it is not without interest to seek the reason why the Colossus was not courageous enough to embark upon such a course. Whether through fear of his actions being wrongly interpreted, or else because he did not feel sure of his ground and was apprehensive lest he might be induced to walk into a trap, Cecil Rhodes never would pronounce himself upon one side or the other. He left to well-wishers the task of reconciliation between himself and his enemies, or, if not that, at least the possibility for both once more to take common action for the solution of South African difficulties. The unfortunate side of the whole affair lay in the fact that the Boer and Bond leaders each remained under the impression that in the Raid affair it was against their particular body that Rhodes had sinned, that it was their cause which he had betrayed. Accordingly they expected him to recognise this fact and to tell them of his regret.

Cecil Rhodes

But this was not Rhodes' way: on the contrary, he looked to his adversaries to consider that they had wronged him. Both parties adhered firmly to their point of view; it was not an easy matter to persuade either of them to take the initiative. Each very well knew and felt it was an indispensable step, but each considered it should be taken by the other.

This brings me to make a remark which probably has never yet found its way into print, though some have spoken about it in South Africa. It is that Cecil Rhodes, whilst being essentially an Empire Maker, was not an Empire Ruler. His conceptions were far too vast to allow him to take into consideration the smaller details of everyday life which, in the management of the affairs of the world, obliges one to consider possible ramifications of every great enterprise. Rhodes wanted simply to sweep away all obstacles without giving the slightest thought to the consequences likely to follow on so offhand a manner of getting rid of difficulties.

In addition to this disregard of vital details, there was a tinge of selfishness in everything which Rhodes undertook and which gave a personal aspect to matters which ought to have been looked upon purely from the objective. The acquisition of Rhodesia, for instance, was considered by him as having been accomplished for the aggrandisement of the Empire and also for his own benefit. He sincerely believed that he had had nothing else in his mind when he founded the Chartered Company, than the desire to conquer a new country and to give it to England; but he would certainly have felt cruelly affronted if the British Government had ever taken its administration into its own hands and not allowed Rhodes to do exactly what he pleased there. He loved to go to Buluwayo, and would spend weeks watching all that was being done in the way of agriculture and mining. In particular, he showed considerable interest in the natives.

The Colonial Office in London was treated by Cecil Rhodes with the utmost disdain on the rare occasions when it tried to put in a word concerning the establishment of British rule in the territories which he gloried in having presented to the Queen. It was sufficient to mention in his presence the possibility of the Charter being recalled to put Rhodes into a passion. No king or tyrant of old, indeed, treated his subjects with the severity which Rhodes showed in regard to the different civil officials and military defenders of the Rhodesia he loved so much and so unwisely.

It is curious that Rhodes never allowed speculation a free hand in Rhodesia as he had done at Kimberley or at Johannesburg. He was most careful that outsiders should not hear about what was going on, and took endless precautions not to expose the companies that worked the old dominions of poor King Lobengula, to the sharp criticism of the European Stock Exchanges. Their shares remained in the hands of people on whose discretion Rhodes believed that he could rely, and no one ever heard of gambling in scrip exciting the minds of the inhabitants of Buluwayo or Salisbury to anything like the degree stocks in Transvaal concerns did.

In Rhodesia Rhodes believed himself on his own ground and free from the criticisms which he guessed were constantly uttered in regard to him and to his conduct. In the new land which bore his name Rhodes was surrounded only by dependants, whilst in Cape Colony he now and then came across someone who would tell him and, what was worse, who would make him feel that, after all, he was not the only man in the world, and that he could not always have everything his own way. Moreover, in Cape Town there was the Governor, whose personality was more important than his own, and whom, whether he liked it or not, he had to take into consideration, and to whom, in a certain sense, he had to submit. And in Kimberley there was the De Beers Board which, though composed of men who were entirely in dependence upon him and whose careers he had made, yet had to be consulted. He could not entirely brush them aside, the less so that a whole army of shareholders stood behind them who, from time to time, were impudent enough to wish to see what was being done with their money.

Nothing in the way of hampering critics or circumscribing authorities existed in Rhodesia. The Chartered Company, though administered by a Board, was in reality left entirely in the hands and under the control of Rhodes. Most of the directors were in England and came before public notice only at the annual general meeting, which was always a success, inasmuch as no one there had ever ventured to criticise, otherwise than in a mild way, the work of the men who were supposed to watch over the development of the resources of the country. Rhodes was master, and probably his power would have even increased had he lived long enough to see the completion of the Cape to Cairo Railway, which was his last hobby and the absorbing interest of the closing years of his life.

The Cape to Cairo Railway was one of those vast schemes that can be ascribed to the same quality in his character as that which made him so essentially an Empire Maker. It was a project of world-wide import-ance, and destined to set the seal to the para-mount influence of Great Britain over the whole of Africa. It was a work which, without Rhodes, would never have been accomplished. He was right to feel proud of having conceived it; and England, too, ought to be proud of having counted among her sons a man capable of starting such a vast enterprise and of going on with it despite the violent opposition and the many misgivings with which it was received by the general public.

CHAPTER VII

RHODES AND THE AFRIKANDER BOND

TO return to the subject of the negotiations which undoubtedly took place between Rhodes and the leaders of the Afrikander Bond during the war, I must say that, so far as I know, they can rank among the most disinterested actions of his life. For once there was no personal interest or possible material gain connected with his desire to bring the Dutch elements in South Africa to look upon the situation from the purely patriotic point of view, as he did himself.

It would have been most certainly to the advantage of everybody if, instead of persisting in a resistance which was bound to collapse, no matter how successful it might appear to have been at its start, the Boers, together with the Dutch Afrikanders, had sent the olive branch to Cape Town. There would then have been some hope of compromise or of coming to terms with England before being crushed by her armies. It would have been favourable to English interests also had the great bitterness, which rendered the war such a long and such a rabid one, not had time to spread all over the country. Rhodes' intervention, which Sir Alfred Milner could not have refused had he offered it, backed by the Boers on one side and by the English Progressive

82

party in the Colony on the other, might have brought about great results and saved many lives.

No blame, therefore, ought to attach to Cecil Rhodes for wishing to present the Boer side of the case. It would, indeed, have been wiser on the part of Mr. Hofmeyr and other Bond leaders to have forgotten the past and given a friendly hand to the one man capable of unravelling the tangled skein of affairs.

At that period, whilst the siege of Kimberley was in progress, it is certain that serious consideration was given to this question of common action on the part of Rhodes and of the two men who practically held the destinies of the Transvaal in their hands—de Wet and General Botha, with Mr. Hofmeyr as representative of the Afrikander Bond at their back. Why it failed would for ever remain a mystery if one did not remember that everywhere in South Africa lurked hidden motives of self-interest which interfered with the best intentions. The fruits of the seed of distrust sown by the Raid were not easy to eradicate.

Perhaps if Mr. Rhodes had stood alone the attempt might have met with more success than was actually the case. But it was felt by all the leading men in the Transvaal that a peace concluded under his auspices would result in the subjection of the Boers to the foreign and German-Jew millionaires. This was the one thing they feared.

The Boers attributed to the millionaires of the Rand all the misfortunes which had fallen upon them, and consequently the magnates were bitterly hated by the Boers. And not without reason. No reasonable Boer would have seriously objected to a union with England, provided it had been effected under conditions assuring them autonomy and a certain independence. But no one wanted to have liberty and fortune left at the mercy of adventurers, even though some of them had risen to reputation and renown, obtained titles, and bought their way into Society.

Unfortunately for him, Rhodes was supposed to represent the class of people referred to, or, at any rate, to favour them. One thing is certain—the great financial interests which Rhodes possessed in the Gold Fields and other concerns of the same kind lent some credence to the idea. All these circumstances prevented public opinion from expressing full confidence in him, because no one could bring himself to believe what nevertheless would have come true.

In the question of restoring peace to South Africa Rhodes most certainly would never have taken anyone's advice; he would have acted according to his own impulse, and more so because Doctor Jameson was not with him during the whole time Kimberley was besieged. Unfortunately for all the parties concerned, Rhodes let slip the opportunity to resume his former friendship with Mr. Hofmeyr, the only man in South Africa whose intelligence could measure itself with his own. And in the absence of this first step from Rhodes, a false pride—which was wounded vanity more than anything else—prevented the Bond from seeking the help of Rhodes. This attitude on the part of each man would simply have been ridiculous under ordinary circumstances, but at a time when such grave interests were at stake, and when the future of so many people was liable to be compromised, it became criminal.

In sharp contrast to it stood the conduct of Sir Alfred Milner, who was never influenced by his personal feelings or by his vanity where the interests of his country were engaged. During the few months which preceded the war he was the object of virulent hatred on the part of most of the white population of the Colony. When the first disillusions of the war brought along with them their usual harvest of disappointments the personality of the High Commissioner appeared at last in its true light, and one began to realise that here was a man who possessed a singularly clear view on matters of politics, and that all his actions were guided by sound principles. His quiet determination not to allow himself to be influenced by the gossip of Cape Town was also realised, and amid all the spite shown it is to his honour that, instead of throwing up the sponge, he persevered, until at last he succeeded in the aim which he had kept before him from the day he had landed in Table Bay. He restored peace to the dark continent where no one had welcomed him, but where everybody mourned his departure when he bade it good-bye after the most anxious years he had ever known.

When Sir Alfred accepted the post of Governor of

the Cape Colony and English High Commissioner in South Africa, he had intended to study most carefully the local conditions of the new country whither fate and his duty were sending him, and then, after having gained the necessary experience capable of guiding him in the different steps he aspired to take, to proceed to the formidable task he had set for himself. His great object was to bring about a reconciliation between the two great political parties in the Colony—the South African League, with Rhodes as President, and the Afrikander Bond, headed by Messrs. Hofmeyr (the one most in popular favour with the Boer farmers), Sauer and Schreiner.

In the gigantic task of welding together two materials which possessed little affinity and no love for each other, Sir Alfred was unable to be guided by his experience in the Motherland. In England a certain constitutional policy was the basis of every party. At the Cape the dominating factors were personal feelings, personal hatreds and affections, while in the case of the League it was money and money alone. I do not mean that every member of the League had been bought by De Beers or the Chartered Company; but what I do maintain is that the majority of its members had some financial or material reason to enrol themselves.

In judging the politics of South Africa at the period of which I am writing, one must not forget that the greater number of those who then constituted the so-called Progressive party were men who had travelled to

Photo: Elliott & Fry

THE HON. J. H. HOFMEYR

the Cape through love of adventure and the desire to enrich themselves quickly. It was only the first comers who had seen their hopes realised. Those who came after them found things far more difficult, and had perforce to make the best of what their predecessors left. On the other hand, it was relatively easy for them to find employment in the service of one or the other of the big companies that sprang up, and by whom most of the mining and industrial concerns were owned.

When the influence of the De Beers increased after its amalgamation with the other diamond companies around Kimberley, and when Rhodes made up his mind that only a political career could help him to achieve his vast plans, he struck upon the thought of using the money and the influence which were at his disposal to transform De Beers into one of the most formidable political instruments the world had ever seen. He succeeded in doing so in what would have been a wonderful manner if one did not remember the crowd of fortune-seeking men who were continually landing in South Africa. These soon found that it would advantage them to enrol under Rhodes' banner, for he was no ordinary millionaire. Here stood a man who was perpetually discovering new treasures, annexing new continents, and who had always at his disposal profitable posts to scatter among his followers.

The reflex action upon Rhodes was that unconsciously he drifted into the conviction that every man could be bought, provided one knew what it was he wanted. He understood perfectly well the art of speculating in his neighbours' weaknesses, and thus liked to invite certain people to make long stays at his house, not because he liked them, but because he knew, if they did not, that they would soon discover that the mere fact of being the guest of Mr. Rhodes procured for them the reputation of being in his confidence.. Being a guest at Groote Schuur endowed a man with a prestige such as no one who has not lived in South Africa can realise, and, furthermore, enabled him to catch here and there scraps of news respecting the money markets of the world, a proper understanding and use of which could be of considerable financial value. A cup of tea at Groote Schuur was sufficient to bring about more than one political conversion.

Once started the South African League soon became a power in the land, not so strong by any means as the Afrikander Bond, but far more influential in official, and especially in financial, circles. Created for the apparent aim of supporting British government in Cape Colony, it found itself almost from the very first in conflict with it, if not outwardly, at least tacitly. After his rupture with the Bond consequent upon the Raid, Rhodes brought considerable energy to bear upon the development of the League. He caused it to exercise all over the Colony an occult power which more than once defied constituted authority, and proved a source of embarrassment to British representatives with greater frequency than they would have cared to own. Sir Alfred Milner, so far as I have been able to see, when taking the reins, had not reckoned upon meeting with this kind of government within a government, and in doing so perhaps did not appreciate its extent. But from the earliest days of his administration it confronted him, at first timidly, afterwards with persistence, and at last with such insolence that he found himself compelled to see what he could do to reduce to impotence this organisation which sought to devour him.

The problem which a situation of the character described thrust upon Sir Alfred was easier to discuss than to solve. The League was a power so wide that it was almost impossible to get rid of its influence in the country. It was controlled by Rhodes, by De Beers, by the Chartered Company, by the members in both Houses who were affiliated to it, by all the great financial establishments throughout South Africa—with but a solitary exception—by the principal industrial and agricultural enterprises in the country. It comprised political men, landowners, doctors, merchants, shipowners, practically all the colonists in Rhodesia, and most of the English residents of the Transvaal. It controlled elections, secured votes, disposed of important posts, and when it advised the Governor the Legislature had to take its remarks into consideration whether or not it approved of them. Under the régime of the days when the League was formed it had been able to develop itself with great facility, the dangers which lurked behind its encroachment on the privileges of the Crown not being suspected. But Sir Alfred Milner discovered the menace at once, and with the quiet firmness and the tact which he always displayed in everything that he undertook proceeded to cope with the organisation.

Sir Alfred soon found himself confronted by the irritation of Rhodes, who had relied on his support for the schemes which he had nursed in regard to the Transvaal. I must here explain the reason why Rhodes had thrown his glances toward the Rand. One must remember the peculiar conditions in which he was placed in being always surrounded by creatures whom he could only keep attached to his person and to his ambition by satisfying their greed for gold. When he had annexed Matabeleland it had been principally in the expectation that one would find there the rich gold-bearing strata said to exist in that region. Unfortunately, this hope proved a fallacious one. Although thousands of pounds were spent in sinking and research, the results obtained were of so insignificant a nature, and the quantity of ore extracted so entirely insufficient to justify systematic exploitation, that the adventurers had perforce to turn their attention toward other fields.

It was after this disillusion that the idea took hold of Rhodes, which he communicated to his friends, to acquire the gold fields of the Rand, and to transform the rich Transvaal into a region where the Chartered Company and the South African League would rule. Previous to this, if we are to believe President Kruger, Rhodes had tried to conclude an alliance with him, and once, upon his return from Beira to Cape Town, had stopped at Pretoria, where he paid a visit to the old Boer statesman.

It is quite likely that on this occasion Rhodes put in a word suggesting that it would be an advantage to the Transvaal to become possessed of an outlet on the seaboard, but I hardly think that Kruger wrote the truth in his memoirs in stating that when mentioning Delagoa Bay Rhodes used the words, "We must simply take it," thus associating himself with Kruger. Cecil Rhodes was far too cute to do any such thing, knowing that it would be interpreted in a sense inimical to his plans. But I should not be surprised if, when the President remarked that Delagoa was Portuguese, he had replied, "It does not matter, and you must simply take it." This would have been far more to the point, as it would have hinted to those who knew how to read between the lines that England, which Rhodes was persuaded was incarnated in himself, would not mind if the Transvaal did lay hands on Delagoa Bay. Such an act would furnish the British Government with a pretext for dabbling to some effect in the affairs of the Transvaal Republic.

Such a move as this would have been just one of these things which Rhodes was fond of doing. He felt sometimes a kind of malicious pleasure in whispering to others the very things likely to get them into trouble should they be so foolish as to do them. In the case of President Kruger, however, he had to deal with a

mind which, though uncouth, yet possessed all the
"slimness" of which so many examples are to be found
in South Africa.

Kruger wrote, "Rhodes represented capital, no
matter how base and contemptible, and whether by
lying, bribery or treachery, all and every means were
welcome to him if they led to the attainment of his ambitious desires." But Oom Paul was absolutely wrong in
thinking that it was the personage he was thus describing
who practised all these abominations. He ought to have
remembered that it was his name only which was associated with all these basenesses, and the man himself,
if left to his better self, would never have condescended
to the many acts of doubtful morality with which his
memory will remain associated in history.

I am firmly convinced that on his own impulse he
would never, for instance, have ventured on the Raid.
But, unhappily, his habit, when something "not quite"
was mentioned to him, was to say nothing and to trust
to his good luck to avoid unpleasant consequences arising
out of his silence. Had he ventured to oppose the
plans of his confederates they would have immediately
turned upon him, and . . . There were, perhaps, past
facts which he did not wish the world to remember. His
frequent fits of raging temper arose from this irksome
feeling, and was his way—a futile way—of revenging
himself on his jailors for the durance in which they kept
him. The man who believed himself to be omnipotent
in South Africa, and who was considered so powerful by

the world at large, was in reality in the hands of the very organisations he had helped to build.

It was not Cecil John Rhodes' will which was paramount in the South African League. Kruger spoke absolutely the truth when he asserted that it was essential "to know something about the Chartered Company before it was possible to realise the true perspective of the history of South Africa during the closing years of the last century." Another of Kruger's sweeping assertions—and one which he never backed by anything tangible—was when he further wrote that Rhodes was "one of the most unscrupulous characters that ever existed, whose motto was 'the end justifies the means,' a motto that contains a creed which represents the whole man." Rhodes by nature was not half so unscrupulous as Kruger himself, but he was surrounded by unscrupulous people, whom he was too indolent to repulse. He was constantly paying the price of his former faults and errors in allowing his name to serve as a shield for the ambitions of those who were in no way worthy of him and who constantly abused his confidence.

The habit became ingrained in the nature of Cecil Rhodes of always doing what he chose without regard to the feelings and sentiments of others. It persisted during the whole of the war, and would probably have proved a serious impediment to the conclusion of peace had he lived until it became accomplished. This characteristic led him, after all his intrigues with the Dutch party and the Bond, to throw himself once more into the arms of the English Progressive party and to start a campaign of his own against the rebel Colonials and the Dutch inhabitants of the Transvaal.

While the siege of Kimberley lasted, even while he was seeking to become reconciled to the British element, Rhodes asserted himself in a strongly offensive manner. He sent to Sir Alfred Milner in Cape Town reports of his own as to the military authorities and dispositions, couched in such alarming tones that the High Commissioner became most uneasy concerning the possible fate of the Diamond City. These reports accused the officers in charge of the town of failing in the performance of their duties, and showing symptoms of abject fear in regard to the besieging Boer army. It was only after an explanation from Sir Redvers Buller, and after the latter had communicated to him the letters which he himself had received from Colonel Kekewich, the commander of the troops to whom had been entrusted the defence of Kimberley, that Sir Alfred was reassured.

The fact was that Rhodes became very impatient to find that his movements were watched by the military authorities, and that sometimes even the orders which he gave for what he considered the greater security of the town, and gave with the superb assurance which distinguished him, were cancelled by the responsible officials. Disgraceful scenes followed. Rhodes was accused of wishing to come to an arrangement with Cronje, who was in charge of the besieging troops, in order to bring the war to an end by his own efforts.

A Military Mandate

I never have been able to ascertain how much of real truth, if any, was in the various accusations made against Cecil Rhodes by the English General Officers, but they were embodied in the message which was alleged to have been flashed across to Kimberley after the battle of Modder River by Lord Methuen, but which was supposed by those whom it concerned to have been inspired by the Commander-in-Chief:

"Tell Mr. Rhodes," the heliograph ran, "that on my entry into Kimberley he and his friends must take their immediate departure."

Two years later, in November, 1902, Sir Redvers Buller, when speaking at the annual dinner of the Devonians in London, remarked that he must protest against the rumours which, during the siege of Kimberley, had been spread by some of its residents that the Imperial authorities had been in a perpetual state of "funk." The allusion was understood to refer to Mr. Rhodes by his partisans, who protested against the speech. Rhodes, indeed, during his whole life was never in greater disfavour with the English Government than after the siege of Kimberley; perhaps because he had always accused Whitehall of not understanding the real state of things in South Africa. The result of that imperative telegram, and Rhodes' belief as to its source, was bitter hatred against Sir Redvers Buller. It soon found expression in vindictive attacks by the whole Rhodesian Press against the strategy, the abilities, and even the personal honesty of Sir Redvers Buller.

Cecil Rhodes

Whether Rhodes, upon his arrival in London, attempted to hurt the General I do not know, but it could be always taken for granted that Rhodes could be a very bad enemy when he chose.

Upon his return to Groote Schuur he seemed more dissatisfied than ever with the Home Government. He was loud in his denunciations and unceasing in his criticisms. Sir Alfred, however, like the wise man he was, preferred to ignore these pinpricks, and invariably treated Rhodes with the utmost courtesy and attention. He always showed himself glad to listen to Rhodes and to discuss with him points which the Colossus thought it worth while to talk over. At that time Rhodes was in the most equivocal position he had ever been in his life. He could not return to Kimberley; he did not care to go to Rhodesia; and in Cape Colony he was always restive.

At this period all kinds of discussions used to take place concerning the ultimate results of the war and the influence which it would have on the future development of affairs in the Transvaal. The financiers began to realise that after the British flag had once been raised at Pretoria they would not have such a good time of it as they had hoped at first, and now, having done their best to hurry on the war, regretted it more than anybody else. The fact was that everybody in South Africa, with the exception of the Boers themselves, who knew very well their own resources, had believed that the war would be over in three months, and that the Transvaal would be transferred into a Crown Colony where adventurers and gold-seekers would have a fine time.

Rhodes himself had more than once expressed his conviction that the destruction of the Boers would not take more than three months at the most, and this assurance was accepted as gospel by most of the financiers of Johannesburg. An exception was Mr. F. Eckstein, the general manager and partner in the concern of Wernher, Beit & Co., and one of the ablest financiers in that city. From the first he was quite pessimistic in regard to the length of time the war would take.

As the war dragged on without there seeming any chance of its being brought to a rapid conclusion, it became evident that England, after all the sacrifices which she was making, would never consent to leave the leaders of the movement—the ostensible object of which had been to grant to the Uitlanders certain privileges to which they had no right—as sole and absolute masters of the situation. In fact, the difficulties of the war made it evident that, once peace was proclaimed, public opinion at home would demand that the Transvaal, together with the Orange Free State, should be annexed to the British Empire in view of a future federation of the whole of South Africa, about which the English Press was already beginning to speak.

That South Africa should not remain a sphere of exploitation sent shivers down the spines of the financiers. The South African League was observed to become quite active in discovering rebels. Their zeal in this direction was felt all over Cape Colony. Their aim was to reduce the register in order to bring about a considerable falling off of voters for the Afrikander Bond, and thereby substantially influence the results of the next election to the Cape Parliament.

At this period certain overtures were made once again to the Bond party. They proceeded apparently from men supposed to act on their own initiative, but who were known to be in favour at Groote Schuur. These advances met with no response, but when the rumour that they had been made spread among the public owing to an indiscretion, Rhodes hastened to deny that he had been a party to the plan—as was his wont when he failed to achieve. All the same, it is a fact that members of the House of Assembly belonging to the Afrikander party visited Groote Schuur in the course of that last winter which Rhodes spent there, and were warmly welcomed. Rhodes showed himself unusually gracious. He hoped these forerunners would rally his former friends to his side once more. But Rhodes was expecting too much, considering all the circumstances. Faithful to his usual tactics, even whilst his Afrikander guests were being persuaded to lend themselves to an intrigue from which they had hoped to win something, Rhodes was making himself responsible for another step likely to render the always strong hatred even more acute than ever. More than that, he was advocating, through certain underground channels, the suspension of the Constitution in Cape Colony.

Photo: Elliott & Fry

THE RT. HON. SIR W. F. HELY-HUTCHINSON

The League and the Bond

The particulars of this incident were only disclosed after the war was over. The whole thing was thrashed out in Parliament and its details communicated to the public by Mr. David de Waal, one of the truest friends Mr. Rhodes ever had. The discussion took place after Sir Alfred Milner had been transferred to Johannesburg and Sir Walter Hely-Hutchinson had taken his place in Cape Town. The South African League had become more active than ever, and was using all its influence to secure a majority for its members at the next general election. The Bond, on its side, had numerous adherents up country, and the stout Dutch farmers had remained faithful to their old allegiance, so there was no hope that they would be induced, even through the influence of money, to give their votes to the Progressives. The only things which remained were: a redistribution of seats, then a clearing out of the register, and, lastly, a suspension of the Constitution, which would have allowed the Governor a "free" hand in placing certain measures on the statute book. The most influential members among the executive of the South African League met at Cotswold Chambers, and Rhodes, who was present, drew up a petition which was to be presented to the Prime Minister. Sir Gordon Sprigg, who filled that office, was a man who, with all his defects, was absolutely incapable of lending himself to any mean trick in order to remain in power. When Sir Gordon became acquainted with the demands of the League he refused absolutely to take a part in what he maintained would have been an everlasting blot on the reputation of the Government.

After Rhodes' death, when the question of the suspension of the Constitution was raised by the Progressives in the House of Assembly, it was discussed in all its details, and it was proved that the South African League, in trying throughout the country to obtain signatures to a monster petition on the matter, had resorted to some more than singular means to obtain these signatures. Mr. Sauer, who was the leader of the Bond party in the Chamber, revealed how the League had employed agents to induce women and sometimes young children to sign the petition, and that at the camp near Sea Point, a suburb of Cape Town, where soldiers were stationed previous to their departure for England, these same agents were engaged in getting them to sign it before they left under the inducement of a fixed salary up to a certain amount and a large percentage after it had been exceeded, according to the number of the names obtained in this way. When trustworthy people of unimpeachable character wrote to the papers denouncing this manœuvre the subsidised papers in Cape Town, and the Rhodesian Press, refused to publish the affidavits sworn on the subject, but wrote columns of calumnies about the Dutch Colonials, and, as a finishing stroke, clamoured for the suspension of the Constitution.

The speech of Mr. Sauer gave rise to a heated debate, during which the Progressive members indignantly denied his assertions. Then stepped in Mr. David de Waal, that friend of Rhodes to whom I have already referred. He rose to bring his testimony to the facts revealed by Mr. Sauer, who was undoubtedly the most able leader which the Afrikander party possessed, with the exception, perhaps, of Mr. Merriman.

"In February, 1902," he said, "there was a meeting in Cotswold Chambers consisting of the twenty-two members of the House of Assembly who went by the name of 'Rhodes' group.' It was at first discussed and ultimately decided to wait on the Prime Minister and to interview him concerning the expenditure of the war, which had reached the sum of £200,000 monthly. Then, after some further discussion, we came to the conclusion to meet once more. This was done on February 17th. You must remember that war was still raging at the time. At this second meeting it was agreed to formulate a scheme to be submitted to the Government which proposed the suspension of the Constitution in regard to five clauses. The first was to be this very suspension, then a new registration of voters, a redistribution of seats, the indemnity to be awarded to the faithful English Colonials, and, finally, the re-establishment of the Constitution. As to this last I must make a statement, and that is, that if I had known that it was meant to withdraw the Constitution for more than one month I would have objected to it, but I was told that it would be only a matter of a few days."

Cecil Rhodes

At this point Mr. de Waal was interrupted by a Progressive member, who exclaimed that Dr. Jameson had denied that such a thing had ever been said or mentioned.

"I know he has done so," replied Mr. de Waal, "but I will make a declaration on my oath. A committee was then appointed," he went on, "which waited on the Prime Minister and presented to him this very same petition. Sir Gordon Sprigg, however, said that he would not be ruled by anyone, because they had a responsible Government. The Committee reported, when it returned, that the Prime Minister was opposed to any movement started on the basis of the petition which they had presented to him, and that he would not move an inch from his declaration, saying energetically, 'Never! I shall never do it!' Sir Gordon Sprigg had further pointed out that the result of such a step would be that the Cape would become a Crown Colony and would find itself in the same position as Rhodesia."

Perhaps this was what Rhodes and the South African League had wished, but the publication of the details connected with this incident, especially proceeding from a man who had never made a secret of the ties which had bound him to Rhodes, and who, among the latter's Dutch friends, had been the only one who had never failed him, drove the first nail into the coffin of Rhodesian politics.

It was common knowledge that de Waal had steadfastly stood by Rhodes even during the terrible time of the Raid. Moreover, he was a man of high integrity, who alone among those who had attached themselves to the destinies of the Empire Maker had never taken part in the financial schemes of a doubtful nature which marked the wonderful career of Rhodes. This declaration opened the eyes of many persons who, to that day, had denied the political intrigues which had been going on at Cotswold Chambers. Afterwards it became relatively easy for Sir Alfred Milner to clear the atmosphere in South Africa and to establish public life on sounder principles than the pure love of gain. It cannot be sufficiently regretted that he should not have done so before Rhodes' death and thus have given Rhodes —and, incidentally, the country for which Rhodes had done so much in the way of material development—the opportunity to shake off his parasites and become a real factor in solidifying the great area in which he was such an outstanding personality.

CHAPTER VIII

THE INFLUENCE OF SIR ALFRED MILNER

THE occult power exercised by the League on the inner politics of South Africa could not fail to impress Sir Alfred Milner most unpleasantly. Frank himself, it must have often been absolutely repulsive to him to have to do with people whom he feared to trust and who believed that they could bring into political life the laxities of the mining camp. Though not aware of it, even before he landed in Cape Town the Progressives had made up their minds to represent him as determined to sweep the Dutch off the face of the earth.

Believing Sir Alfred to be the confederate of Rhodes, the Boers, too, would have nothing to do with him. Whilst the Bloemfontein Conference was going on President Kruger, as well as the leaders of the Afrikander Bond, were overwhelmed with covert warnings to distrust the High Commissioner. Whence they emanated is not a matter of much doubt. Sir Alfred was accused of wanting to lay a trap for the Boer plenipotentiaries, who were told to beware of him as an accomplice of Mr. Joseph Chamberlain, whose very name produced at Pretoria the same effect as a red rag upon a bull. Under these circumstances the Conference was bound to fail, and the High Commissioner returned to Cape Town, very decidedly a sadder and most certainly a wiser man.

Now that years have passed since the Boer War it is possible to secure a better perspective, in the light of which one can question whether it would have been possible to avoid the conflict by an arrangement of some kind with the Boer Republics. Personally, I believe that an understanding was not out of the question if the strong financial interests had not opposed its accomplishment; but at the same time a patched up affair would not have been a happy event for either South Africa or for England. It would have left matters in almost the same condition as they had been before, and the millionaires, who were the real masters on the Rand, would have found a dozen pretexts to provoke a new quarrel with the Transvaal Government. Had the Boer Executive attempted to do away with the power of the concerns which ruled the gold mines and diamond fields, it would have courted a resistance with which it would have been next to impossible to deal. The war would still have taken place, but it might have occurred at a far less favourable moment. No arrangement with President Kruger, even one most propitious to British interests, could have done away with the corruption and the bribery which, from the first moment of the discovery of the gold fields, invaded that portion of South Africa, and this corruption would always have stood in the way of the establishment of the South African Union.

Cecil Rhodes

Sir Alfred Milner knew all this very well, and probably had an inward conviction, notwithstanding his efforts to prevent the war, that a conflict was the only means of breaking these chains of gold which shackled the wheels of progress. At so critical a time the support of Rhodes and his party would have been invaluable. And Sir Alfred would have welcomed it. Cecil Rhodes, of course, had declared himself officially in accord with the High Commissioner, and even praised him to a degree of fulsomeness. But the ulterior motive was simply to excite the Dutch party against him. The reputation of Sir Alfred Milner as a statesman and as a politician was constantly challenged by the very people who ought to have defended it. Rhodes himself had been persuaded that the Governor harboured the most sinister designs against his person. The innuendo was one of the most heinous untruths ever invented by his crowd of sycophants.

An opportunity came my way, by which I was able to convince myself how false was the belief nourished by Rhodes against Milner. During the course of a conversation with Sir Alfred, I boldly asked him whether he was really such an enemy of Rhodes as represented. I was surprised by the moderate tone in which he replied to my, after all, impertinent question. The remarks which we then exchanged filled me with the greatest admiration for the man who so nobly, and so worthily, upheld British prestige in South Africa under the most trying circumstances. Milner was an entirely honest man—the rarest thing in the whole of Cape Town at that anxious period—and after one had had the advantage of discussing with him the political situation, one could only be filled with profound respect for him and for his opinions, actions and conduct. Far from working against Rhodes, as Sir Alfred had been represented to me as doing, I convinced myself that he was keenly anxious to be on good and, what is more important, on sincere terms with him. Sir Alfred had not the slightest feeling of animosity against the Dutch. On the contrary, he would have liked them to become persuaded of his desire to protect them against possible aggression by the Jingoes, whose offensive conduct none more than himself assessed at its true value.

But what was the real situation? He found his every action misconstrued; whatever he did was interpreted in a wrong sense, and those who should have shared his aims were plotting against him. The position was truly tragic from whatever side it was viewed, and a weaker or less honest man would assuredly have given up the struggle.

A few days after my conversation with Sir Alfred Milner, which took place during the course of a dinner at Government House, I took opportunity to mention it to Rhodes. I tried to clear his mind of the suspicions that I knew he entertained in regard to the High Commissioner. Cecil Rhodes listened to me with attention, then asked me in that sarcastic tone of his, which was so intensely disagreeable and offensive, whether I was in love with Sir Alfred, as I had so suddenly become his champion. Then he ended, "You are trying to make me believe the impossible." I did not allow him, however, to ruffle me, as evidently was his desire, but replied that when one came to know better those whom one had only met occasionally, without ever having talked with them seriously, it was natural to amend one's opinion accordingly. I told him, too, that my earlier misapprehension had been intensified by a certain lady who posed as Rhodes' greatest friend, and who had been loud in her denunciations of the High Commissioner, long before I had ever met him. But now, I added, I had come to the conclusion that Sir Alfred had been terribly maligned.

At this point Rhodes interrupted me with the remark: "So you think that he is a paragon. Well, I won't contradict you, and, besides, you know that I have always defended him; but still, with all his virtues, he has not yet found out what he ought to do with me."

"What can one do with you, Mr. Rhodes?" I asked with a smile.

"Leave me alone," was the characteristic reply, in a tone which was sufficient for me to follow the advice, as it meant that the man was getting restive and might at any moment break out into one of those fits of rage which he so often used as a means to bring to an end a conversation in which he felt that he might not come out as victor.

A few days later a rabid Rhodesian who happened

to be staying at Groote Schuur approached me. " You have been trying to convert Mr. Rhodes to Sir Alfred," he remarked.

" I have done nothing of the kind," I said. " I am not a preacher, but I have been telling Mr. Rhodes that he was mistaken if he thought that he had an enemy in the High Commissioner."

" Had you any reason to suppose that he considered him one? " was the unexpected question.

" Well, from what I have seen it seemed to me that you have all been doing your best to persuade him that such was the case," I retorted, " and why you should have done so passes my comprehension."

The conversation dropped, but the incident confirmed me in my opinion that strong forces were at work to sow enmity between Rhodes and Sir Alfred Milner for fear the influence of the High Commissioner might bring Rhodes to look at things differently. As things stood at the moment, Rhodes was persuaded that the High Commissioner hated him, was jealous of him, wanted him out of his path, and never meant to allow him under any circumstances whatever to have any say in the settlement of South African affairs. This conviction, which was carefully nourished from the outside, evoked in his mind an absurd and silly rage to which no man of common sense, unblinded by vanity, could have fallen victim. I would not be so foolish as to deny to the famous Life Governor of De Beers either abundant common sense or outstanding intelligence, but here was a man gifted with genius who, under the impulse of passion, could act and speak like a child.

Rhodes looked upon the High Commissioner as a nuisance unfortunately not to be set aside. What exasperated him, especially in regard to the High Commissioner, was the fact that he knew quite well that Sir Alfred Milner could assume the responsibility for concluding peace when that time arrived. Rhodes always hoped that his personal influence on the English, as well as among the Bond party, would enable him to persuade the leaders of the rebel movement in Cape Colony to lay down their arms and to leave their interests in his hands. Should such a thing have happened, Rhodes thought that such a success as this would efface the bad impression left by the Raid. He grudgingly admitted that that wild adventure had not pleased people, but he always refused to acknowledge that it was the one great and unredeemable mistake of his life. I remember once having quoted to him the old French motto which in the Middle Ages was the creed of every true knight:

> "*Mon âme à Dieu,*
> *Mon bras au roi,*
> *Mon cœur aux dames,*
> *L'honneur à moi!*"

"Ah, yes! In those times one could still think about such things," he simply remarked, which proved to me that he had no comprehension of the real sense of the beautiful words. The higher attributes of mind

A Man of Earth and Sky

did not trouble him either in the hours of his greatest triumphs or in the moments when Fortune ceased to smile upon him. He thought he had something far better: ambition, love of domination, the desire to eclipse everybody and everything around him. I do not mention money, because Rhodes did not care for money intrinsically.

Yet the man was great in spite of all his defects. Particularly in the rein he gave to his thoughts during nights spent in the solitude of the karroo, when the stars were almost the only things which he could look upon, their immensity the only companion worthy of himself. One could almost believe Cecil Rhodes was possessed of a dual personality. At one moment he lived in the skies in regard to his own future prospects and the great deeds he wished to perform, about which he never ceased to think. The next he was on this earth, dabbling in the meannesses of humanity, taking a vicious pleasure in noticing the evil about him and too frequently succeeding, somehow, in wounding the feelings of those who liked him best, and then wondering how it happened that he had so few friends.

On account of these characteristics, notwithstanding all his wonderful faculties, Cecil Rhodes will never remain an historical figure like the Count of Egmont during the Revolt of the Netherlands, or Mirabeau at the time of the French Revolution. Undoubtedly he achieved great things, but nothing truly beautiful. I do not think that even the warmest of his admirers can ever say that the organising and amalgamation of De Beers or the conquest of Matabeleland had anything beautiful about them. Still, they were triumphs which no one except himself could have achieved. He undoubtedly erected an edifice the like of which had never been seen in modern times, and he opened to the ambitions and to the greed of the world new prospects, new sources of riches, which caused very many to look upon him as truly the god of material success.

Rhodes can be said to have revolutionised Society by bringing to the social horizon people who, but for the riches he placed within reach of their grasping fingers, would never have been able to emerge from their uncultured obscurity.

People have said to me, "How generous was Rhodes!" Yes, but always with a shade of disdain in the giving which hurt the recipients of his charity. One of the legends in the Cape is that half those whom Rhodes helped had been his victims at one time or the other.

It was no wonder that Cecil Rhodes was an embittered man when one reflects how many curses must have been showered upon his head. The conquest of Matabeleland had not gone by without evoking terrible enmities; and the amalgamation of De Beers, in consequence of which so many people who had spent thousands of pounds in acquiring plots of ground where they had hoped to find diamonds, and who had later to part from them for a mere song, were among the things never forgiven him by those whom the speculations had ruined. Later on came the famous Bill which he caused to be adopted in both Houses of Legislature concerning the illicit buying of diamonds, the I.D.B. Act.

The I.D.B. enactment destroyed one of the fundamental principles in British legislature which always supposes a man to be innocent until he has been proved guilty. It practically put the whole of Cape Colony under the thumb of De Beers. The statute was not wisely framed. It could be invoked to remove persons whose presence in Kimberley was inconvenient. Therefore the I.D.B. Act drew on the head of Rhodes and of his colleagues torrents of abuse. It is, unfortunately, certain that cases happened where diamonds were hidden surreptitiously among the effects of certain persons who had had the imprudence to say too loudly that they meant to expose the state of things existing in Kimberley; and in consequence innocent men were sentenced to long terms of imprisonment.

I heard one story in particular which, if true, throws a terrible light on the state of affairs in the Diamond City. A young man of good connections, who had arrived from England to seek his fortune in South Africa, was engaged in Kimberley at a small salary by one of the big diamond mining concerns. After about three or four months' sojourn he felt so disgusted that he declared quite loudly that as soon as he could put by sufficient money to pay his passage back to Europe he would do so, there to make it the business of his life to enlighten his compatriots as to what was going on in South Africa. He threatened, too, to warn his country-men against those who used to deluge England with prospectuses praising, in exalted terms, the wonderful state of things existing in South Africa and dilating upon the future prospects of Cape Colony. Old resi-dents warned him he would do better to restrain his wrath until he was out of reach of interested parties; he did not listen to them, with the result that one morning detectives appeared in the house where he lodged, searched his room, and—found some diamonds hid-den in a flower pot of geraniums which was standing in his window and which the daughter of his landlady had given him that very morning. No protestations of the unhappy young fellow availed him. He was taken to Cape Town and condemned to seven years' imprison-ment, the end of which he did not live to see, as he died a few months after he had been sentenced.

The story was freely current in South Africa; and, true or not, it is unquestionable that a large number of persons suffered in consequence of the I.D.B. Act, no more serious proofs being offered that they had taken or concealed diamonds than the fact that the stones had been found in unlikely places in their rooms. Books without number have been written about the I.D.B. Act, a great number evidently evincing hatred or revenge against Mr. Rhodes and his lieutenants.

The famous De Beers Company acquired a position of overwhelming strength in the social, economical and political life of South Africa, where practically it secured control of everything connected with finance and industry. De Beers built cold storage rooms, a dynamite factory, ice houses, interested itself in agriculture, fruit-growing, farming and cattle-breeding all over the Colony. It managed to acquire shares in all the new mining enterprises whether in the Transvaal or in Rhodesia. Politically it controlled the elections, and there were certain districts in the Cape Colony where no candidate unsupported by De Beers could hope to be elected to a seat in Parliament. The company had its own police, while its secret service was one of the most remarkable in the world, having among its archives a record of the private opinions of all the people enjoying any kind of eminence in the country. In presence of De Beers the Governor himself was overshadowed; indeed, I do not think that if the Home Government had tried to oppose the organisation it would have had much chance of coming out on top.

Sir Alfred Milner was the first man who saw that it would be impossible for England to have the last word in South Africa unless those who, both in Cape Colony and in the Transvaal, were the real masters of the situation were broken, and financial concerns persuaded to occupy themselves solely with financial matters. Though Sir Alfred was wise enough, and prudent enough, not to allow his feelings on the subject to become public property, Rhodes was shrewd enough to guess that he would encounter a resolute adversary in the person of

the High Commissioner. Perhaps had he kept his suspicions to himself instead of communicating them to
others he might have been persuaded in time to recognise that there was a great deal in the opinions which
Sir Alfred held as to the participation of financial organisations in political matters. If only each could have had
a chance for a frank understanding, probably Milner
would not have objected to Rhodes continuing to control the vast machine into which the diamond mines
amalgamation had grown, so long as it confined its operations to commerce.

If Government is exercised by a single person it is
possible for it to possess the elements of justice and
equity, and to be carried out with few mistakes of such
gravity as would compromise the whole system. But,
unfortunately, the South African autocracy meant an
army of small autocrats, and it was they who compromised
Rhodes and then sheltered themselves behind his gigantic
personality from the unpopularity and detestation which
their actions aroused in the whole of South Africa.

I feel personally convinced that if, during the period
which immediately followed upon the relief of Kimberley and of Ladysmith, Rhodes had approached Sir
Alfred and frankly told him that he wanted to try his
luck with the Dutch party, and to see whether his former
friends and colleagues of the Afrikander Bond could not
be induced to listen to reason, the High Commissioner
would have been only too glad to meet him and to
explain his views on the whole question. Instead of

doing so, Rhodes, carried away as he always was by this everlasting desire to be the first everywhere, did not even give a thought to the wisdom of confiding to any-one the efforts which he undoubtedly made to induce the Bond leaders to trust him again.

There was a moment when things got very near to an understanding between Rhodes and Sir Alfred. This was when Mr. Sauer himself entertained the thought of letting Rhodes sway the future by making with the English Government conditions of a peace which would not wound to the quick the feelings of the Dutch part of the population of the Colony.

A circumstance, apparently insignificant, destroyed all the hopes that had been entertained by several who wished the Colossus well. Certain papers were brought to Rhodes; these contained information likely to prove of use to him as well as to the English Government. After he had read them he asked that they should be left with him until the following day. The person in charge of the documents had been asked not to part with them even for a single hour, as it was important that no one should be able to copy documents which might seriously compromise certain people. Therefore, she re-fused. Rhodes thereupon flew into a terrible passion and demanded to know the reason for the apparent dis-trust. When told that it was not so much a question of distrust as the impossibility of breaking a promise once given, he exclaimed that he would have nothing more to do with the whole business, and started almost immediately afterwards his agitation for the suspension of the Constitution in Cape Colony. But—and this is an amusing detail to note—Rhodes used every possible effort to obtain possession of the papers he had been allowed to see, going so far as to have the house searched of the person who had refused to allow him to keep the documents—a revenge which was as mean as it was useless, because the papers in question had been at once returned to their rightful owners.

The request made by Rhodes to keep these documents produced a very bad impression on those who had begun to entertain hopes that he might be induced to throw the weight of his personality into the scale of a settlement. It confirmed the suspicions held by the Afrikander party ever since the Raid.

They say that everyone is afforded once the chance of one's lifetime. In the case of Rhodes, he certainly missed by that action the one opportunity of reinstating himself once again upon the pinnacle whence the adventure of Doctor Jameson had caused him to fall.

I remember that whilst these events were going on a political man, well acquainted with all details of the endeavour to secure a reconciliation between the Afrikander Bond and Rhodes, came to see me one evening. We talked over the whole situation. He told me that there were people who thought it would be a good thing to inform Sir Alfred Milner of what was going on, in the hope that he might give Rhodes an inkling that he knew that intrigue was rife at Groote Schuur, and at

A Plan which Misfired

the same time express to Rhodes with what satisfaction he personally would view the good offices of the Colossus to influence both the South African League and the Afrikander Bond. But we agreed that it was quite impossible. Such a course would not inspire the High Commissioner with an exalted idea as to our morality in matters of trust, and, besides, it would not be playing the game in regard to Rhodes and his group. So the matter dropped; but Rhodes suspected, and never forgave us or any of those whose thoughts ran on the same lines.

Whether Sir Alfred Milner ever learned who had been trying to persuade the master of Groote Schuur to seek his co-operation in what would have been the noblest deed of Rhodes' life, I have not been able to ascertain to the present day. To tell the truth, I never tried to do so, the matter having lost all interest except as a matter of history.

CHAPTER IX

THE OPENING OF THE NEW CENTURY

SUCH were the preoccupations, the intrigues and the emotions which, all through that monotonous winter of 1900-1901, agitated the inhabitants of and the visitors to Groote Schuur. Rhodes himself seemed to be the one man who thought the least about them. It is certain that he felt hurt in his pride and in his consciousness that the good which he had wanted to do failed to be appreciated by those whom he had intended to benefit. But outwardly he made no sign that the matter interested him otherwise than from a purely objective point of view, that of the statesman who thinks that it is part of his duty to put his services at the disposal of his country whenever required to do so. He felt also slightly surprised to find, once he had expressed his willingness to use the experience of South African affairs which he had acquired and which no one in the Cape possessed with such thoroughness, that the people who had appealed to him, and whom he had consented to meet half-way, would not give him the whole of their confidence; indeed, they showed some apprehension that he would use his knowledge to their detriment.

When one reviews all the circumstances that cast such a tragic shade over the history of these eventful months, one cannot help coming to the conclusion that there was a good deal of misunderstanding on both sides and a deplorable lack of confidence everywhere. Rhodes had entirely lost ground among his former friends, and would not understand that it was more difficult, even on the part of those who believed in his good intentions, to efface the impression that he had been playing a double game ever since the Raid had deprived him of the confidence and support which previously were his all over Cape Colony.

The whole situation, as the new century opened, was a game of cross purposes. Sir Alfred Milner might have unravelled the skein, but he was the one man whom no one interested in the business wished to ask for help. And what added to the tragedy was the curious but undisputable fact that even those who reviled Rhodes hoped he would return to power and assume the Premiership in place of Sir Gordon Sprigg.

In spite of the respect which Sir Gordon Sprigg inspired, and of the esteem in which he was held by all parties, it was generally felt that if Rhodes were once more at the helm he might return to a more reasonable view of the whole situation. In such an office, too, it was believed that Rhodes would give the Colony the benefit of his remarkable gifts of statecraft, as well as wield the authority which he liked so much to exercise, for the greater good of the country in general and of the British Government in particular. I believe that if at that moment Cecil Rhodes had become the head of the Cabinet not one voice, even among the most fanatic of the Afrikander Bond, would have objected. Those most averse to such a possibility were Rhodes' own supporters, a small group of men whose names I shall refrain from mentioning.

All true friends of Rhodes, however, must surely have felt a keen regret that he wasted his talents and his energy on those entangled and, after all, despicable Cape politics. The man was created for something better and healthier than that. He was an Empire Maker by nature, one who might have won for himself everlasting renown had he remained "King of Rhodesia," as he liked to call himself. There, in the vast solitudes which by his enterprise and foresight had become a part of the British Empire, he ought to have gone on uninterruptedly in the glorious task of bringing civilisation to that hitherto unknown land. For such work his big nature and strange character were well fitted, and his wide-ranging mind appreciated the extent of the task. As he used to say himself sometimes, he was never so happy and never felt so free and so much at peace with the world and with mankind as among the Matoppo Hills.

The statesmanlike qualities which Cecil Rhodes undoubtedly possessed were weakened by contact with inferior people. It is impossible to create real politicians and sound ones at the same rapid pace as financial magnates sprang up at the Cape as well as in the Transvaal. The class who entered politics had as little real solidity about them as the houses and dwellings which were built at a moment's notice from corrugated iron and a few logs. They thought that they understood how to govern a nation because they had thoroughly mastered the mysteries of bookkeeping in problematical financial undertakings.

I remember one afternoon when, talking with Rhodes in the grounds of Groote Schuur, he took me to the summer-house which he had built for himself, whence one had a beautiful view over the country toward Table Mountain. He leaned on the parapet of the little observatory which surmounted the summer-house and lost himself in a day dream which, though long, I felt I had better not interrupt. I can see his face and expression still as, with his arms crossed over his chest, he gazed into space, thinking, thinking, and forgetting all else but the vision which he was creating in that extraordinary brain of his. I am sure that he remained so for over twenty minutes. Then he slowly turned round to me and said, with an accent indescribable in its intensity and poignancy :

"I have been looking at the North, at my own country——"

"Why do you not always remain there?" I exclaimed almost involuntarily, so painfully did the words strike me.

"Because they will not let me," he replied.

"They? Who?" I asked again. "Surely you can do what you like?"

"You think so," he said, "but you do not know;

there are so many things; so many things. And they want me here too, and there is this place . . ."

He stopped, then relapsed once more into his deep meditation, leaving me wondering what was holding back this man who was reputed to do only what he chose. Surely there would have been a far better, far nobler work for him to do there in that distant North which, after all, in spite of the beauties of Groote Schuur, was the only place for which he really cared. There he could lead that absolutely free and untrammelled life which he loved; there his marvellous gifts could expand with the freedom necessary for them to shine in their best light for the good of others as well as for his own advantage. In Rhodesia he was at least free, to a certain extent, from the parasites.

How could one help pitying him and regretting that his indomitable will did not extend to the courage of breaking from his past associations; that he did not carry his determination far enough to make up his mind to consecrate what was left of his life to the one task for which he was best fitted, that of making Rhodesia one of the most glorious possessions of the British crown. Rhodes had done so much, achieved so much, had conceived such great things—as, for instance, the daring inception of the Cape to Cairo Railway—that it surely could have been possible for him to rise above the shackling weaknesses of his environment.

So many years have passed since the death of Rhodes that, now, one can judge him objectively. To me, knowing him so well as I did, it seem that as his figure recedes into the background of history, it acquires more greatness. He was a mystery to so many because few had been able to guess what it was that he really meant, or believed in, or hoped for. Not a religious man by any means, he yet possessed that religion of nature which pervades the soul of anyone who has ever lived for long face to face with grandeurs and solitudes where human passions have no entrance. It is the adoration of the Greatness Who created the beauty which no touch can defile, no tongue slander, and nobody destroy. Under the stars, to which he confided so much of the thoughts which he had kept for himself in his youth and early manhood, Rhodes became a different man. There in the silence of the night or the dawn of early morning, when he started for those long rides of which he was so fond, he became affectionate, kind, thoughtful and tender. There he thought, he dreamt, he planned, and the result of these wanderings of his mind into regions far beyond those where the people around him could stray was that he revealed himself as God had made him and such as man hardly ever saw him.

Rhodes had always been a great reader; books, indeed, had a great influence over his mind, his actions and opinions. He used to read slowly, and what he had once assimilated he never forgot. Years after he would remember a passage treating of some historical fact, or of some social interest, and apply it to his own work. For instance, the idea of the Glen Grey Act was suggested to him by the famous book of Mackenzie Wallace dealing with Russia,* in which he described the conditions under which Russian peasants then held their land. When Rhodes met the author of the aforementioned volume at Sandringham, where both were staying with the then Prince and Princess of Wales, he told him at once, with evident pleasure at being able to do so, that it was his book which had suggested that particular bit of legislation.

Another occasion I remember when Rhodes spoke of the great impression produced upon his opinions by a book called " The Martyrdom of Man,"† the work of Winwood Reade, an author not very well known to the general public. The essay was an unusually powerful negation of the Divinity. Rhodes had, unfortunately for him, chanced across it just after he had left the University, and during the first months following upon his arrival in South Africa he read it in his moments of leisure between looking for diamonds in the sandy plains of Kimberley. It completely upset all the traditions in which he had been nurtured—it must be remembered that he was the son of a clergyman—and caused a revolt against the teachings of his former masters.

The adventurous young man who had left his native country well stocked with principles which he was already beginning to find embarrassing, found in

* "Russia" (Cassell).
† Published in the U.S.A., 1875.

this volume an excuse for becoming the personage with whom the world was to become familiar later on, when he appeared on the horizon as an Empire Maker. He always kept this momentous book beside him, and used to read it when he wanted to strengthen himself in some hard resolution or when he was expected to steel his mind to the performance of some task against which his finest instincts revolted even whilst his sense of necessity urged him onward.

Talking with me on the occasion I have referred to above, in respect to this volume which had left such weeds in his mind, he expressed to me his great enthusiasm about the ideas it contained, and spoke with unmeasured approval of its strong and powerful arguments against the existence of a Deity, and then exclaimed, "You can imagine the impression which it produced on me when I read it amid all the excitement of life at Kimberley not long after leaving Oxford University." And he added in a solemn tone, "That book has made me what I am."

I think, however, that Rhodes exaggerated in attaching such influence to Reade's essay. He was very interested in the supernatural, a feature which more than once I have had occasion to observe in people who pretend that they believe in nothing. I suspect that, had he been able to air the doubts which must have assailed him sometimes when alone in the solitudes of Rhodesia, one would have discovered that a great deal of carelessness, of which he used to boast in regard to

127

morality and to religion, was nothing but affectation. He treated God in the same offhand way he handled men, when, in order to terrify them, he exposed before their horrified eyes abominable theories, to which his whole life gave the lie. But in his inmost heart he knew very well that God existed. He would have felt quite content to render homage to the Almighty if only this could have been done incognito. In fact, he was quite ready to believe in God, but would have felt extremely sorry had anyone suspected that such could be the case.

The ethical side of Cecil Rhodes' character remained all through his life in an unfinished state. It might perhaps have been the most beautiful side of his many-sided life had he not allowed too much of what was material, base and common to rule him. Unwillingly, perhaps, but nevertheless certainly, he gave the impression that his life was entirely dedicated to ignoble purposes. Perhaps the punishment of his existence lay precisely in the rapidity with which the words." Rhodesian finance" and "Rhodesian politics" came to signify corruption and bribery. Even though he may not have been actually guilty of either, he most certainly profited by both. He instituted in South Africa an utter want of respect for one's neighbour's property, which in time was a prime cause of the Transvaal War. Hated as he was by some, distrusted as he remained by almost everybody, yet there was nothing mean about Cecil Rhodes. Though one felt inclined to detest him at times, yet one could not help liking and even loving him when he allowed one to see the real man behind the veil of cynicism and irony which he constantly assumed.

With Rhodes' death the whole system of Rhodesian politics perished. It then became relatively easy for Sir Alfred Milner to introduce the necessary reforms into the government of South Africa. The financial magnates who had ruled at Johannesburg and Kimberley ceased to interest themselves politically in the management of the affairs of the Government. They disappeared one after the other, bidding good-bye to a country which they had always hated, most of them sinking into an obscurity where they enjoy good dinners and forget the nightmare of the past.

The Dutch and the English elements have become reconciled, and loyalty to England, which seemed at the time of the Boer War, and during the years that had preceded it, to have been confined to a small number of the English, has become the rule. British Imperialism is no mere phantom: the Union of South Africa has proved it to have a very virile body, and, what is more important, a lofty and clear-visioned soul.

CHAPTER X

AN ESTIMATE OF SIR ALFRED MILNER

THE conditions under which Sir Alfred Milner found himself compelled to shape his policy of conciliation were beset with obstacles and difficulties. An understanding of these is indispensable to the one who would read aright the history of that period of Imperial evolution.

The question of the refugees who overwhelmed Cape Colony with their lamentations, after they had been obliged to leave the Transvaal at the beginning of the hostilities—the claims of the Rand multi-millionaires— the indignation of the Dutch Colonists confined in concentration camps by order of the military authorities—the Jingoes who thought it would be only right to shoot down every Dutch sympathiser in the country : these were among the things agitating the South African public mind, and setting up conflicting claims impossible of adjustment without bitter censure on one hand or the other. The wonder is that, amid all these antagonistic elements, Sir Alfred Milner contrived to fulfil the larger part of the tasks which he had sketched out for himself before he left England.

The programme which Sir Alfred planned to carry out proved, in the long run, to have been thoroughly sound in conception and practice, because it contained in embryo all the conditions under which South Africa became united. It is remarkable, indeed, that such a very short time after a war which seemed altogether to have compromised any hope of coalescing, the Union of South Africa should have become an accomplished fact.

Yet, strange as it may appear, it is certain that up to his retirement from office Sir Alfred Milner was very little known in South Africa. He had been so well compelled by force of circumstances to lead an isolated life that very few had opportunity to study his character or gain insight into his personality. In Cape Town he was judged by his policy. People forgot that all the time he was at Government House, Cape Town, he was a man as well as a politician: a man whose efforts and work in behalf of his country deserved some kind of consideration even from his enemies. It is useless to discuss whether Sir Alfred did or did not make mistakes before the beginning of the war. Why waste words over events which cannot be helped, and about which there will always be two opinions? Personally, I think that his errors were essentially of the kind which could not have been avoided, and that none of them ever compromised ultimately the great work which he was to bring to a triumphant close.

What I do think it is of value to point out is the calmness which he contrived always to preserve under circumstances which must have been particularly trying for him. Another outstanding characteristic was the quiet dignity with which he withstood unjustifiable attacks when dealing with not-to-be-foreseen difficulties which arose while carrying on his gigantic task. Very few would have had the courage to remain silent and undaunted whilst condemned or judged for things he had been unable to alter or to banish. And yet this was precisely the attitude to which Sir Alfred Milner faithfully adhered. It stands out among the many proofs which the present Viscount Milner has given of his strong character as one of its most characteristic features, for it affords a brilliant illustration of what will, mastered by reason, can do.

Since those perilous days I have heard many differing criticisms of Lord Milner's administration as High Commissioner in South Africa. What those who express opinions without understanding that which lies under the surface of history fail to take into account is the peculiar, almost invidious position and the loneliness in which Sir Alfred had to stand from the very first day that he landed in Table Bay. He could not make friends, dared not ask anyone's advice, was forced always to rely entirely upon his own judgment. He would not have been human had he not sometimes felt misgivings as to the wisdom of what he was doing. He never had the help of a Ministry upon whom he could rely or with whom he could sympathise. The Cabinet presided over by Sir Gordon Sprigg was composed of very well-intentioned men. But, with perhaps one single exception, it did not possess any strongly individualistic personage capable of

Photo : Russell

VISCOUNT MILNER

assisting Sir Alfred in framing a policy acceptable to all shades of public opinion in the Colony, or even to discuss with him whether such a policy could have been invented. As for the administration of which Mr. Schreiner was the head, it was distinctly hostile to the policy inaugurated by Mr. Joseph Chamberlain, which Sir Alfred represented. Its members, indeed, put every obstacle in the Governor's way, and this fact becoming known encouraged a certain spirit of rebellion among the Dutch section of the population. Neither one Ministry nor the other was able to be of any serious use to Milner, who, thus hampered, could neither frame a programme which accorded with his own judgment nor show himself in his true light.

All these circumstances were never taken into consideration by friends or foes, and, in consequence, he was made responsible for blunders which he could not help and for mistakes which he was probably the first to deplore. The world forgot that Sir Alfred never really had a free hand, was always thwarted, either openly or in secret, by some kind of authority, be it civil or military, which was in conflict with his own.

It was next to an impossibility to judge a man fairly under such conditions. All that one could say was that he deserved a good deal of praise for having, so successfully as he did, steered through the manifold difficulties and delicate susceptibilities with which he had to contend in unravelling a great tangle in the history of the British Empire.

Cecil Rhodes

The Afrikander Bond hated him, that was a recognised fact, but this hatred did Sir Alfred more good than anything else. The attacks directed against him were so mean that they only won him friends among the very people to whom his policy had not been acceptable. The abuse showered by certain newspapers upon the High Commissioner not only strengthened his hands and his authority, but transformed what ought to have remained a personal question into one in which the dignity as well as the prestige of the Empire was involved. To have recalled him after he had been subjected to such treatment would have been equivalent to a confession that the State was in the wrong. I have never been able to understand how men of such undoubted perception as Mr. Sauer or Mr. Merriman, or other leaders of the Bond, did not grasp this fact. Sir Alfred himself put the aspect very cleverly before the public in an able and dignified speech which he made at the lunch offered to Lord Roberts by the Mayor and Corporation of Cape Town when he said, " To vilify her representative is a strange way to show one's loyalty to the Queen."

A feature in Sir Alfred Milner's character, which was little known outside the extremely small circle of his personal friends, was that when he was in the wrong he never hesitated to acknowledge the fact with straightforward frankness. His judgments were sometimes hasty, but he was always willing to amend an opinion on just grounds. There was a good deal of dogged firmness in his character, but not a shred of stubbornness or obstinacy. He never yielded one inch of his ground when he believed himself to be in the right, but he was always amenable to reason, and he never refused to allow himself to be convinced, even though it may be that his natural sympathies were not on the side of those with whom he had got to deal. Very few statesmen could boast of such qualities, and they surely ought to weigh considerably in the balance of any judgment passed upon Viscount Milner.

The welfare of South Africa and the reputation of Sir Alfred would have been substantially enhanced had he been able to assert his own authority according to his own judgment, without overrulings from Whitehall, and with absolute freedom as to choice of colleagues. His position was most difficult, and though he showed no outward sign of this fact, it is impossible to believe that he did not feel its crushing weight. Between the Bond, Mr. Hofmeyr, the race hatred which the Dutch accused him of fomenting, the question of the refugees, the clamours of the Jingo Colonials, and the extreme seriousness of the military situation at one time, it was perfectly marvellous that he did not break down. Instead, as very few men could have done, he kept a clear-headed shrewdness, owing to which the Empire most certainly contracted an immense debt of gratitude toward him for not having allowed himself to yield to the temptation of retaliating upon those who had made his task such a particularly hard one. His forbearance ought

135

never to be lost sight of in judging the circumstances which brought about and attended the South African War. Whilst the war was going on it was not realised that Sir Alfred Milner was the only man who—when the time arrived—could allay the passions arising from the conflict. But, without vanity, he knew, and could well afford to wait for his reward until history rather than men had judged him.

In the meanwhile Sir Alfred had to struggle against a sea of obstacles in which he was probably the only man clever enough not to drown himself—a danger which overtook others who had tried to plunge into the complicated politics of South Africa. A succession of administrators at Government House in Cape Town ended their political career there, and left, broken in spirit, damaged in reputation.

As for the local politicians, they were mostly honest mediocrities or adventurous spirits, who used their influence for their personal advantage. An exception was Mr. Hofmeyr. But he was far too absorbed in securing the recognition of Dutch supremacy at the Cape to be able to work on the milder plane necessary to bring about the one great result. The popularity of Mr. Hofmeyr was immense and his influence indisputable; but it was not a broad influence. He shuddered at the mere possibility of the Transvaal falling into the hands of the British.

Whilst touching upon the subject of the Transvaal, I may say a word concerning the strangely mixed popu-

Racial Classifications

lation, for the sake of whom, officially, Britain went to war. The war was entirely the work of the Uitlanders, as they called themselves with a certain pride, but very few of whom possessed a drop of English blood. The British public at home was told that it was necessary to fight President Kruger because Englishmen in the Transvaal were being ill-treated and denied their legitimate rights. In reality, this was one of those conventional reasons, lacking common sense and veracity, upon which nations are so often fed. If we enter closely into the details of existence in the Transvaal, and examine who were those who shouted so loudly for the franchise, we find that the majority were either foreigners or Jews hailing from Frankfurt or Hamburg. Many of them had, to be sure, become naturalised British subjects, but I doubt very much whether, among all the magnates of Johannesburg or of Kimberley, more than one or two pure-blooded Englishmen could be found. Rhodes, of course, was an exception, but one which confirmed the rule. Those others whose names can still be conjured with in South Africa were Jews, mostly of Teutonic descent, who pretended that they were Englishmen or Colonials; nothing certain was known about their origin beyond the fact that such or such small shops in Grahamstown, Durban or Cape Town had witnessed their childish romps. The Beits, the Neumanns and the Wernhers were German Jews; Barney Barnato was supposed to have been born under the shade of a Portuguese synagogue, and considered the fact as being just as glorious

137

a one as would have been that of having in his veins "all the blood of all the Howards." The Joels were Hebrews; the Rudds supposed to belong to the same race through some remote ancestor; the Mosenthals, Abrahams, Phillipps, and other notabilities of the Rand and Kimberley, were Jews, and one among the so-called Reformers, associated with the Jameson Raid, was an American engineer, John Hays Hammond.

The war, which was supposed to win the franchise for Englishmen in the Transvaal, was in reality fought for the advantage of foreigners. Most people honestly believed that President Kruger was aiming at destroying English prestige throughout the vast dark continent, and would have been horrified had they known what was going on in that distant land. Fortunes were made on the Rand in a few days, but very few Englishmen were among the number of those who contrived to acquire millions. Englishmen, indeed, were not congenial to the Transvaal, whilst foreigners, claiming to be Englishmen because they murdered the English language, abounded and prospered, and in time came sincerely to believe that they were British subjects, owing to the fact that they continually kept repeating that Britain ought to possess the Rand.

When Britain came really to rule the Rand the adventurers found it did not in the least secure the advantages which they had imagined would derive from a war they fostered. This question of the Uitlanders was as embarrassing for the English Government as it had been for that of the Transvaal. These adventurers, who composed the mass of the motley population which flourished on the Rand, would prove a source of annoyance to any State in the world. On the other hand, the importance acquired by the so-called financial magnates was daily becoming a public danger, inasmuch as it tended to substitute the reign of a particular class of individuals for the ruling of those responsible for the welfare of the country. These persons individually believed that they each understood better than the Government the conditions prevailing in South Africa, and perpetually accused Downing Street of not realising and never protecting British interests there.

Amidst their recriminations and the publicity they could command from the Press, it is no wonder that Sir Alfred Milner felt bewildered. It is to his everlasting honour that he did not allow himself to be overpowered. He was polite to everybody; listened carefully to all the many wonderful tales that were being related to him, and, without compromising himself, proceeded to a work of quiet mental elimination that very soon made him thoroughly grasp the intricacies of any situation. He quickly came to the conclusion that President Kruger was not the principal obstacle to a peaceful development of British Imperialism in South Africa. If ever a conflict was foisted on two countries for mercenary motives it was the Transvaal War, and a shrewd and impartial mind like Milner's did not take long to discover that such was the case.

Cecil Rhodes

He was not, however, a man capable of lending himself meekly to schemes of greed, however wilily they were cloaked. His was not the kind of nature that for the sake of peace submits to things of which it does not approve. This man, who was represented as an oppressor of the Dutch, was in reality their best friend, and perhaps the one who believed the most in their eventual loyalty to the English Crown. It is a thousand pities that when the famous Bloemfontein Conference took place Sir Alfred Milner, as he still was at that time, had not yet acquired the experience which later became his concerning the true state of things in the Transvaal. Had he at that time possessed the knowledge which he was later to gain, when the beginning of hostilities obliged so many of the ruling spirits of Johannesburg to migrate to the Cape, it is likely that he would have acted differently. It was not easy for the High Commissioner to shake off the influence of all that he heard, whether told with a good or bad intention, and it was still harder for him in those first days of his office to discern who was right or who was wrong among those who crowded their advice upon him—and never forgave him when he did not follow their ill-balanced counsels.

Concerning the outstanding personality of Cecil Rhodes, the position of Sir Alfred Milner was even more difficult and entangled than in regard to anyone else. It is useless to deny that he had arrived at Cape Town with considerable prejudice against Rhodes. He could not but look interrogatively upon the political career of a man who at the very time he occupied the position of Prime Minister had lent himself to a conspiracy against the independence of another land. Moreover, Rhodes was supposed, perhaps not without reason, to be continually intriguing to return to power, and to be chafing in secret at the political inaction which had been imposed upon him, and for which he was himself responsible more than anyone else. The fact that after the Raid Rhodes had been abandoned by his former friends harmed him considerably as a political man by destroying his renown as a statesman to whom the destinies of an Empire might be entrusted with safety. One can truly say, when writing the story of those years, that it resolved itself into the vain struggle of Rhodes to recover his lost prestige. Sir Alfred was continually being made responsible for things of which he had not only been innocent, but of which, also, he had disapproved most emphatically. To mention only one—the famous concentration camps. A great deal of fuss was made about them at the time, and it was generally believed that they had been instituted at the instigation of the High Commissioner. When consulted on the subject Sir Alfred Milner had, on the contrary, not at all shared the opinion of those who had believed that they were a necessity, although ultimately, for lack of earlier steps, they became so.

The Colony at that time found its effective government vested in the hands of the military authorities, who not infrequently acted upon opinions which were not based upon experience or upon any local conditions. They believed, too, implicitly what they were told, and when they heard people protest, with tears in their eyes, their devotion to the British Crown, and lament over the leniency with which the Governor of Cape Colony looked upon rebellion, they could not possibly think that they were listening to a tissue of lies, told for a purpose, nor guess that they were being made use of. Under such conditions the only wonder is the few mistakes which were made. To come back to the Boers' concentration camps, Sir Alfred Milner was not a sanguinary man by any means, and his character was far too firm to use violence as a means of government. It is probable that, left alone, he would have found some other means to secure strict obedience from the refugees to orders which most never thought of resisting. Unfortunately for everybody concerned, he could do nothing beyond expressing his opinion, and the circumstance that, out of a feeling of duty, he made no protestations against things of which he could not approve was exploited against him, both by the Jingo English party and by the Dutch, all over South Africa. At Groote Schuur especially, no secret was made by the friends of Rhodes of their disgust at the state of things prevailing in concentration camps, and it was adroitly brought to the knowledge of all the partisans of the Boers that, had Rhodes been master of the situation, such an outrage on individual liberty would never have taken place. Sir Alfred Milner was subjected to unfair, ill-natured criticisms which were as cunning as they were bitter. The concentration camps afford only one instance of the secret antagonisms and injustices which Sir Alfred Milner had to bear and combat. No wonder thoughts of his days in South Africa are still, to him, a bitter memory!

CHAPTER XI

CROSS CURRENTS

THE intrigues which made Groote Schuur such a disagreeable place were always a source of intense wonder to me. I could never understand their necessity. Neither could I appreciate the kind of hypocrisy which induced Rhodes continually to affirm that he did not care to return to power, whilst in reality he longed to hold the reins again. It would have been fatally easy for Rhodes, even after the hideous mistake of the Raid, to regain his political popularity; a little sincerity and a little truth were all that was needed. Unfortunately, both these qualities were wanting in what was otherwise a really gifted nature. Rhodes, it seemed by his ways, could not be sincere, and though he seldom lied in the material sense of the word, yet he allowed others to think and act for him, even when he knew them to be doing so in absolute contradiction to what he ought to have done himself. He appeared to have insufficient energy to enforce his will on those whom he despised, yet allowed to dictate to him even in matters which he ought to have kept absolutely under his own control.

I shall always maintain that Rhodes, without his so-called friends, would most certainly have been one of the greatest figures of his time and generation. He had

A Warped Outlook

a big soul, vast conceptions, and when he was not influenced by outward material details—upon which, unfortunately for himself as well as for his reputation in history, he allowed his mind to dwell too often—his thoughts were always directed toward some higher subject which absorbed his attention, inspired him, and moved him sometimes to actions that drew very near to the heroic. He might have gone to his grave not only with an unsullied, but also with a great reputation based on grounds that were noble and splendid had he shaken off the companions of former times. Unhappily, an atmosphere of flattery and adulation had become absolutely necessary to him, and he became so used to it that he did not perceive that his sycophants never left him alone for a moment. They watched over him like a policeman who took good care no foreign influence should venture to approach.

The end of all this was that Rhodes resented the truth when it was told him, and detested any who showed independence of judgment or appreciation in matters concerning his affairs and projects. A man supposed to have an iron will, yet he was weak almost to childishness in regard to these flattering satellites. It amused him to have always at his beck and call people willing and ready to submit to his insults, to bear with his fits of bad temper, and to accept every humiliation which he chose to offer.

Cecil Rhodes never saw, or affected never to see, the disastrous influence all this had on his life.

Cecil Rhodes

I remember asking him how it came that he seldom showed the desire to go away somewhere quite alone, if even for a day or two, so as to remain really tête-à-tête with his own reflections. His reply was most characteristic: "What should I do with myself? One must have people about to play cards in the evening." I might have added "and to flatter one," but refrained. This craving continually to have someone at hand to bully, scold, or to make use of, was certainly one of the failings of Rhodes' powerful mind. It also indicated in a way that thirst for power which never left him until the last moment of his life. He had within him the weakness of those dethroned kings who, in exile, still like to have a Court about them and to travel in state. Rhodes had a court, and also travelled with a suite who, under the pretence of being useful to him, effectually barred access to any stranger. But for his entourage it is likely that Rhodes might have outlived the odium of the Raid. But, as Mrs. van Koopman said to me, "What is the use of trying to help Rhodes when one is sure that he will never be allowed to perform all that he might promise?"

The winter which followed upon the relief of Kimberley Rhodes spent almost entirely at Groote Schuur, going to Rhodesia only in spring. During these months negotiations between him and certain leaders of the Bond party went on almost uninterruptedly. These were either conducted openly by people like Mr. David de Waal, or else through other channels when not entrusted to persons whom it would be relatively easy later on to disavow. Once or twice these negotiations seemed to take a favourable turn at several points, but always at the last minute Rhodes withdrew under some pretext or other. What he would have liked would have been to have, as it were, the Dutch party, the Bond, the English Colonists, the South African League, President Kruger, and the High Commissioner, all rolled into one, fall at his feet and implore him to save South Africa. When he perceived that all these believed that there existed a possibility for matters to be settled without his intervention, he hated every man of them with a hatred such as only very absolute natures can feel. To hear him express his disgust with the military authorities, abuse in turns Lord Roberts, whom he used to call an old man in his dotage, Lord Kitchener, who was a particular antipathy, the High Commissioner, the Government at home, and the Bond, was an education in itself. He never hesitated before making use of an expression of a coarseness such as does not bear repeating, and in his private conversations he hurled insults at the heads of all. It is therefore no wonder that the freedom of speech which Rhodes exercised at Groote Schuur added to the difficulties of a situation the brunt of which not he, but Sir Alfred Milner, had to bear.

More than once the High Commissioner caused a hint to be conveyed to Cecil Rhodes that he had better betake himself to Rhodesia, and remain there until there

was a clearer sky in Cape Colony. These hints were
always given in the most delicate manner, but Rhodes
chose to consider them in the light of a personal affront,
and poured down torrents of invective upon the British
Government for what he termed their ingratitude. The
truth of the matter was that he could not bring himself to understand that he was not the person alone
capable of bringing about a permanent settlement of
South Africa. The energy of his young days had left
him, and perhaps the chronic disease from which he was
suffering added to his constant state of irritation and
obscured the clearness of his judgment in these post-
raid days.

I hope that my readers will not imagine from my
reference that I have a grudge of any kind against
Doctor Jameson.* On the contrary, truth compels me
to say that I have seldom met a more delightful creature
than this old friend and companion of Cecil Rhodes,
and I do believe he held a sincere affection for his chief.
But Jameson, as well as Rhodes, was under the influence of certain facts and of certain circumstances, and
I do not think that he was, at that particular moment
about which I am writing, the best adviser that Rhodes
might have had. In one thing Doctor Jim was above
suspicion : he had never dirtied his hands with any of
the financial speculations which those about Rhodes
indulged in, to the latter's detriment much more than
his own, considering the fact that it was he who was

* Dr. Jameson died November 26th, 1917.

Photo: Ball

THE RT. HON. SIR LEANDER STARR JAMESON

considered as the father of their various "smart" schemes. Jameson always kept aloof from every kind of shady transaction in so far as money matters were concerned, and perhaps this was the reason why so many people detested him and kept advising Rhodes to brush him aside, or, at all events, not to keep him near him whilst the war was going on. His name was to the Dutch as a red rag to a very fierce and more than furious bull, while the Bond, as well as the burghers of the Transvaal, would rather have had dealings with the Evil One himself than with Doctor Jim. Their prejudices against him were not to be shaken. In reality others about Rhodes were far more dangerous than Jameson could ever have proved on the question of a South African settlement in which the rights of the Dutch elements in the Cape and Orange Free State would be respected and considered.

Whatever might have been his faults, Doctor Jameson was neither a rogue nor a fool. For Rhodes he had a sincere affection that made him keenly alive to the dangers that might threaten the latter, and anxious to avert them. But during those eventful months of the war the influence of the Doctor also had been weakened by the peculiar circumstances which had arisen in consequence of the length of the Boer resistance. Before the war broke out it had been generally supposed that three months would see the end of the Transvaal Republic, and Rhodes himself, more often than I care to remember, had prophesied that a few weeks would be the utmost that the struggle could last. That this did not turn out to be the case had been a surprise to the world at large and an intense disappointment to Cecil Rhodes. He had all along nourished a bitter animosity against Kruger, and in regard to him, as well as Messrs. Schreiner, Merriman, Hofmeyr, Sauer and other one-time colleagues, he carried his vindictiveness to an extent so terrible that more than once it led him into some of the most regrettable actions in his life.

Cecil Rhodes possessed a curious shyness which gave to his character an appearance the more misleading in that it hid in reality a will of iron and a ruthlessness comparable to a *Condottiere* of the Middle Ages. The fact was that his soul was thirsting for power, and he was inordinately jealous of successes which anyone but himself had or could achieve in South Africa. I am persuaded that one of the reasons why he always tried by inference to disparage Sir Alfred Milner was his annoyance at the latter's calm way of going on with the task which he had mapped out for himself without allowing his mind to be troubled by the outcries of a mob whom he despised from the height of his great integrity, unsullied honour, and consciousness of having his duty to perform. Neither could Rhodes ever see in political matters the necessities of the moment often made it the duty of a statesman to hurl certain facts into oblivion and to reconcile himself to new circumstances.

That he did disparage Sir Alfred Milner is unfortunately certain. I sincerely believe that the war would never have dragged on so long had not Rhodes contrived to convey to the principal Boer leaders the impression that while Sir Alfred Milner remained in South Africa no settlement would be arrived at with the British Government, because the High Commissioner would always oppose any concessions that might bring it to a successful and prompt issue. Of course Cecil Rhodes never said this in so many words, but he allowed people to guess that such was his conviction, and it was only after Sir Alfred had left the Cape for Pretoria that, by a closer contact with the Boers themselves, some of the latter's prejudices against him vanished.

At last did the sturdy Dutch farmers realise that if there was one man devoid of animosity against them, and desirous of seeing the end of a struggle which was ruining a continent, it was Sir Alfred Milner. They also discovered another thing concerning his political views and opinions—that he desired just as much as they did to destroy the power and influence of those multi-millionaires who had so foolishly believed that after the war's end they would have at their disposal the riches which the Transvaal contained, so that, rather than becoming a part of the British Empire, it would in reality be an annexe of the London and Paris Stock Exchanges.

As events turned out, by a just retribution of Providence, the magnates who had let greedy ambition master them lost most of the advantages which they had been able to snatch from President Kruger. Whether this would have happened had Rhodes not died before the conclusion of peace remains an open question. It is certain he would have objected to a limitation of the political power of the concerns in which he had got such tremendous interests; it is equally sure that it would have been for him a cruel disappointment had his name not figured as the outstanding signature on the treaty of peace. There were in this strange man moments when his patriotism assumed an entirely personal shape, but, improbable as it may appear to the reader, there was sincerity in the conviction which he had that the only man who understood what South Africa required was himself, and that in all that he had done he had been working for the benefit of the Empire. There was in him something akin to the feeling which had inspired the old Roman saying, "*Civis Romanum sum.*" He understood far better than any of the individuals by whom he was surrounded the true meaning of the word Imperialism. Unfortunately, he was apt to apply it in the personal sense, until, indeed, it got quite confused in his mind with a selfish feeling which prompted him to put his huge personality before everything else. If one may do so, a reading of his mind would show that in his secret heart he felt he had not annexed Rhodesia to the Empire nor amalgamated the Kimberley mines and organised De Beers for the benefit of his native Britain, but in order to make himself the most powerful man in South Africa, and yet at the same time shrewdly realised that he could not be the king he wished to become unless England stood behind him to cover with her flag his heroic actions as well as his misdeeds.

That Rhodes' death occurred at an opportune moment cannot be denied. It is a sad thing to say, but for South Africa true enough. It removed from the path of Sir Alfred Milner the principal obstacle that had stood in his way ever since his arrival at Cape Town. The Rhodesian party, deprived of its chief, was entirely harmless. Rhodesian politics, too, lost their strength when he was no longer there to impose them upon South Africa.

One of the great secrets of the enormous influence which the Colossus had acquired lay in the fact that he had never spared his money when it was a question of thrusting his will in directions favourable to his interest. None of those who aspired to take his place could follow him on that road, because none were so superbly indifferent to wealth. Cecil Rhodes did not care for riches for the personal enjoyments they can purchase. He was frugal in his tastes, simple in his manners and belongings, and absolutely careless as to the comforts of life. The waste in his household was something fabulous, but it is a question whether he ever participated in luxuries showered upon others. His one hobby had been the embellishment of Groote Schuur, which he had really transformed into something absolutely fairylike as regards its exterior beauties and the loveliness of its grounds and gardens. Inside, too, the house, furnished after the old Dutch style, struck one by its handsomeness, though it was neither homelike nor comfortable. In its decoration he had followed the plans of a clever architect, to whose artistic education he had generously contributed by giving to him facilities to travel in Europe, but he had not lent anything of his own personality to the interior arrangements of his home, which had always kept the look of a show place, neither cared for nor properly looked after.

Rhodes himself felt happier and more at his ease when rambling in his splendid park and gazing on Table Mountain from his stoep than amidst the luxury of his richly furnished rooms. Sometimes he would sit for hours looking at the landscape before him, lost in a meditation which but few cared to disturb, and after which he invariably showed himself at his best and in a softer mood than he had been before. Unfortunately, these moments never lasted long, and he used to revenge himself on those who had surprised him in such reveries by indulging in the most caustic and cruel remarks which he could devise in order to goad them out of all patience. A strange man with strange instincts; and it is no wonder that, once, a person who knew him well, and who had known him in the days of his youth when he had not yet developed his strength of character, had said of him that "One could not help liking him and one could not avoid hating him; and sometimes one hated him when one liked him most."

Sir Alfred Milner had neither liked nor hated him,

perhaps because his mind was too well balanced to allow him to view him otherwise than with impartiality and with a keen appreciation of his great qualities. He would have liked to work with Rhodes, and would gladly have availed himself of his experience of South Africa and of South African politicians. But Sir Alfred refused to be drawn into any compromises with his own conscience or to offend his own sense of right and wrong. He was always sincere, though he was never given credit for being so in South Africa. Sir Alfred Milner could not understand why Rhodes, instead of resolutely asserting that he wanted to enter into negotiations with the Bond in order to win its co-operation in the great work of organising the new existence of South Africa on a sound and solid basis, preferred to cause promises to be made to the Bond which he would never consent to acknowledge.

These tortuous roads, which were so beloved by Rhodes, were absolutely abhorrent to the High Commissioner. When Rhodes started the agitation for the suspension of the Constitution, which occupied his thoughts during the last months of his life—an agitation whch he had inaugurated out of spite against Mr. Sauer and Mr. Hofmeyr, who had refused to dance to Rhodes' tune—Sir Alfred Milner had at once seen through the underlying motives of the moment, and what he discerned had not increased his admiration for Rhodes. Sir Alfred had not opposed the plans, but he had never been sanguine as to their chance of success, and they were not in accordance with his own convictions. Had he thought they had the least chance of being adopted, most certainly he would have opposed them with just as much energy as Sir Gordon Sprigg had done. He saw quite well that it would not have been opportune or politic to put himself into open opposition to Rhodes. Sir Alfred therefore did not contradict the rumours which attributed to him the desire to reduce the Cape to the condition of a Crown Colony, but bent his energy to the far more serious task of negotiating a permanent peace with the leading men in the Transvaal, a peace for which he did not want the protection of Rhodes, and to which an association with Rhodes might have proved inimical to the end in view—the ideal of a South African Federation which Rhodes had been the first to visualise, but which Providence did not permit him to see accomplished.

CHAPTER XII

THE CONCENTRATION CAMPS

IT is impossible to speak or write about the South African War without mentioning the Concentration Camps. A great deal of fuss was made about them, not only abroad, where all the enemies of England took a particular and most vicious pleasure in magnifying the so-called cruelties which were supposed to take place, but also in the English Press, where long and heart-rending accounts appeared concerning the iniquities and injustices practised by the military authorities on the unfortunate Boer families assembled in the Camps.

In recurring to this long-forgotten theme, I must first of all say that I do not hold a brief for the English Government or for the administration which had charge of British interests in South Africa. But pure and simple justice compels me to protest, first against the use which was made for party purposes of certain regrettable incidents, and, more strongly still, against the totally malicious and ruthless way in which the incidents were interpreted.

It is necessary before passing a judgment on the Concentration Camps to explain how it came about that these were organised. At the time of which I am writing people imagined that by Lord Kitchener's orders Boer women, children and old people were forcibly taken away from their homes and confined, without any reason for such an arbitrary proceeding, in unhealthy places where they were subjected to an existence of privation as well as of humiliation and suffering. Nothing of the kind had taken place.

The idea of the Camps originated at first from the Boers themselves in an indirect way. When the English troops marched into the Orange Free State and the Transvaal, most of the farmers who composed the bulk of the population of the two Republics having taken to arms, there was no one left in the homes they had abandoned save women, children and old men no longer able to fight. These fled hurriedly as soon as English detachments and patrols were in sight, but most of the time they did not know where they could fly to, and generally assembled in camps somewhere on the veldt, where they hoped that the British troops would not discover them. There, however, they soon found their position intolerable owing to the want of food and to the lack of hygienic precautions.

The British authorities became aware of this state of things and could not but try to remedy it. Unfortunately, this was easier said than done. To come to the help of several thousands of people in a country where absolutely no resources were to be found was a quite stupendous task, of a nature which might well have caused the gravest anxieties to the men responsible for the solution. It was then that the decision was reached to organise upon a reasonable scale camps after the style of those which already had been inaugurated by the Boers themselves.

The idea, which was not a bad one, was carried out in an unfortunate manner, which gave to the world at large the idea that the burgher families who were confined in these camps were simply put into a prison which they had done nothing to deserve. The Bond Press, always on the alert to reproach England, seized hold of the establishment of the Camps to transform into martyrs the persons who had been transferred to them, and soon a wave of indignation swept over not only South Africa, but also over Britain. This necessary act of human civilisation was twisted to appear as an abuse of power on the part of Lord Roberts and especially of Lord Kitchener, who, in this affair, became the scapegoat for many sins he had never committed. The question of the Concentration Camps was made the subject of interpellations in the House of Commons, and indignation meetings were held in many parts of England. The Nonconformist Conscience was deeply stirred at what was thought to be conduct which not even the necessities of war could excuse. Torrents of ink were spilt to prove that at the end of the nineteenth century measures and methods worthy of the Inquisition were resorted to by British Government officials, who—so the ready writers and ready-tongued averred—with a barbarity such as the Middle Ages had not witnessed, wanted to be revenged on innocent women

159

and children for the resistance their husbands and fathers were making against an aggression which in itself nothing could justify.

So far as the Boers themselves were concerned, I think that a good many among them viewed the subject with far more equanimity than the English public. For one thing, the fact of their women and children being put in places where at least they would not die of hunger must have come to them rather in the light of a relief than anything else. Then, too, one must not lose sight of the conditions under which the Boer burghers and farmers used to exist in normal times. Cleanliness did not rank among their virtues; and, as a rule, hygiene was an unknown science. They were mostly dirty and neglected in their personal appearance, and their houses were certainly neither built nor kept in accordance with those laws of sanitation which in the civilised world have become a matter of course. Water was scarce, and the long and torrid summers, during which every bit of vegetation was dried up on the veldt, had inured the population to certain privations which would have been intolerable to Europeans. These things, and the unfortunate habits of the Boers, made it extremely difficult, if not impossible, to realise in the Camps any approach to the degree of cleanliness which was desirable.

To say that the people in the Concentration Camps were happy would be a gross exaggeration, but to say that they were martyrs would convey an equally false idea. When judging of facts one ought always to remember the local conditions under which these facts have developed. A Russian moujik sent to Siberia does not find that his life there is very much different from what it was at home, but a highly civilised, well-educated man, condemned to banishment in those frozen solitudes, suffers acutely, being deprived of all that had made existence sweet and tolerable to him. I feel certain that an Englishman, confined in one of the Concentration Camps of South Africa, would have wished himself dead ten times a day, whilst the wife of a Boer farmer would not have suffered because of missing soap and water and clean towels and nicely served food, though she might have felt the place hot and unpleasant, and might have lamented over the loss of the home in which she had lived for years.

The Concentration Camps were a necessity, because without them thousands of people, the whole white population of a country indeed, amounting to something over sixty thousand people, would have died of hunger and cold.

The only means of existence the country Boers had was the produce of their farms. This taken away from them, they were left in the presence of starvation, and starvation only. This population, deprived of every means of subsistence, would have invaded Cape Colony, which already was overrun with white refugees from Johannesburg and the Rand, who had proved a prolific source of the greatest annoyance to the British

Government. To allow this mass of miserable humanity to wander all over the Colony would have been inhuman, and I would like to know what those who, in England and upon the Continent, were so indignant over the Concentration Camps would have said had it turned out that some sixty thousand human creatures had been allowed to starve.

The British Government, owing to the local conditions under which the South African War came to be fought, found itself in a dilemma, out of which the only escape was to try to relieve wholesale misery in the most practical manner possible. There was no time to plan out with deliberation what ought to be done; some means had to be devised to keep a whole population alive whom an administration would have been accused of murdering had there been delay in feeding it.

There was also another danger to be faced had the veldt been allowed to become the scene of a long-continued migration of nations—that of allowing the movements of the British troops to become known, thereby lengthening a war of already intolerable length, to say nothing of exposing uselessly the lives of English detachments, which, in this guerrilla kind of warfare, would inevitably have occurred had the Boer leaders remained in constant communication with their wandering compatriots.

Altogether the institution of the Concentration Camps was not such a bad one originally. Unfortunately, they were not organised with the seriousness which ought to have been brought to bear on such a delicate matter, and their care was entrusted to people who succeeded, unwittingly perhaps, in making life there less tolerable than it need have been.

I visited some of the Concentration Camps, and looked into their interior arrangements with great attention. The result of my personal observations was invariably the same—that where English officials were in charge of these Camps everything possible was done to lighten the lot of their inmates. But where others were entrusted with surveillance, every kind of annoyance, indignity and insult was offered to poor people obliged to submit to their authority.

In this question, as in many others connected with the Boer War, it was the local Jingoes who harmed the British Government more than anything else, and the Johannesburg Uitlanders, together with the various Volunteer Corps and Scouts, brought into the conduct of the enterprises with which they were entrusted an intolerance and a smallness of spirit which destroyed British prestige far more than would have done a dozen unfortunate wars. The very fact that one heard these unwise people openly say that every Boer ought to be killed, and that even women and children ought to be suppressed if one wanted to win the war, gave abroad the idea that England was a nation thirsting for the blood of the unfortunate Afrikanders. This mistaken licence furnished the Bond with the pretext to persuade the Dutch Colonists to rebel, and the Boer leaders with that of going on with their resistance until their last penny had been exhausted and their last gun had been captured.

Without these detestable Jingoes, who would have done so much harm not only to South Africa, but also to their Mother Country, England, it is certain that an arrangement, which would have brought about an honourable peace for everybody, could have come much sooner than it did. A significant fact worth remembering—that the Boers did not attempt to destroy the mines on the Rand—goes far to prove that they were not at all so determined to hurt British property, or to ruin British residents, or to destroy the large shareholder concerns to which the Transvaal owed its celebrity, as was credited to them.

When the first rumours that terrible things were going on in the Concentration Camps reached England there were found at once amateurs willing to start for South Africa to investigate the truth of the accusations. A great fuss was made over an appeal by Lady Maxwell, the wife of the Military Governor of Pretoria, in which she entreated America to assist her in raising a fund to provide warm clothing for the Boer women and children. Conclusions were immediately drawn, saddling the military authorities with responsibility for the destitution in which these women and children found themselves. But in the name of common sense, how could one expect that people who had run away before what they believed to be an invasion of barbarians determined to burn down and destroy all their belongings—how could one expect that these people in their flight would have thought about taking with them their winter clothes, which, in the hurry of a departure in a torrid summer, would only have proved a source of embarrassment to them? More recently we have seen in Belgium, France, Poland and the Balkans what occurred to the refugees who fled before foreign invasion. The very fact of Lady Maxwell's appeal proved the solicitude of the official English classes for the unfortunate Boers and their desire to do something to provide them with the necessaries of life.

Everybody knows the amount of money which is required in cases of this kind, and—in addition to America's unstinting response—public and private charity in Britain flowed as generously as it always does upon every occasion when an appeal is made to it in cases of real misfortune. But when it comes to relieve the wants of about sixty-three thousand people, of all ages and conditions, this is not so easy to do as persons fond of criticising things which they do not understand are apt sweepingly to declare. Very soon the question of the Concentration Camps became a Party matter, and was made capital of for Party purposes without discrimination or restraint. Sham philanthropists filled the newspapers with their indignation, and a report was published in the form of a pamphlet by Miss Hobhouse, which, it is to be feared, contained some percentage of tales poured into her ears by people who were nurtured in the general contempt for truth which at that time existed in South Africa.

If the question of Concentration Camps had been examined seriously, it would have been at once perceived what a tremendous burden the responsibility of having to find food and shelter for thousands of enemy people imposed on English officials. No one in Government circles attempted or wished to deny, sorrowful as it was to have to recognise it, that the condition of the Camps was not, and indeed could not be, nearly what one would have wished or desired. On the other hand, the British authorities were unremitting in their efforts to do everything which was compatible with prudence to improve the condition of these Camps. Notwithstanding, people were so excited in regard to the question, and it was so entirely a case of "Give a dog a bad name," that even the appointment of an Imperial Commission to report on the matter failed to bring them to anything approaching an impartial survey. Miss Hobhouse's report had excited an emotion only comparable to the publication of Mrs. Beecher Stowe's famous novel, "Uncle Tom's Cabin."

Miss Hobhouse came to South Africa inspired by the most generous motives, but her lack of knowledge of the conditions of existence common to everyone in that country prevented her from forming a true opinion as to the real hardship of what she was called upon to witness. Her own interpretations of the difficulties and discomforts which she found herself obliged to face proved that she had not realised what South Africa really was. Her horror at the sight of a snake in one of the tents she visited could only evoke a smile from those who had lived for some time in that country, as a visitor of that particular kind was possible even in the suburbs of Cape Town, and certainly offered nothing wonderful in a tent on the high veldt. The same remark can be applied to the hotels, which Miss Hobhouse described as something quite ghastly. Everyone who knew what South Africa really was could only agree with her that the miserable places there were anything but pleasant residences, but the fuss which she made as to these trivial details could only make one sceptical as to the genuineness of the other scenes which she described at such length. No one who had had occasion to watch the development of the war or the circumstances which had preceded it could bring himself to believe with her that the British Government was guilty of premeditated cruelty.

Of course, it was quite dreadful for those who had been taken to the Concentration Camps to find themselves detained there against their will, but at the same time, as I have already remarked, the question remains as to what these people would have done had they been left absolutely unprotected and unprovided for among the remnants of what had once been their homes. It was certain that Miss Hobhouse's pamphlet revealed a parlous state of things, but did she realise that wood, blankets, linen and food were not things which could be transported with the quickness that those responsible heartily desired? Did she remember that the British troops also had to do without the most elementary comforts, in spite of all the things which were constantly being sent from home for the benefit of the field forces? Both had in South Afica two enemies in common that could not be subdued—distance and difficulty of communication. With but a single line of railway, which half the time was cut in one place or another, it was but natural that the Concentration Camps were deprived of a good many things which those who were compelled to live within their limits would, under different circumstances or conditions, have had as a matter of course.

Miss Hobhouse had to own that she met with the utmost courtesy from the authorities with whom she had to deal, a fact alone which proved that the Government was only too glad to allow people to see what was being done for the Boer women and children, and gratefully appreciated every useful suggestion likely to lighten the sad lot of those in the Camps.

It is no use denying, and indeed no one, Sir Alfred Milner least of all, would have denied that some of the scenes witnessed by Miss Hobhouse, which were afterwards described with such tremulous indignation, were of a nature to shock public opinion both at home and abroad. But, at the same time, it was not fair to circumstances or to people to have a false sentimentality woven into what was written. Things ought to have

A Libel

been looked upon through the eyes of common sense and not through the refracting glasses of the indignation of the moment. It was a libel to suggest that the British authorities rendered themselves guilty of deliberate cruelty, because, on the contrary, they always and upon every occasion did everything they could to lighten the lot of the enemy peoples who had fallen into their hands.

CHAPTER XIII

THE PRISONERS' CAMPS

I WENT myself very carefully into the details of whatever information I was able to gather in regard to the treatment of Boer prisoners in the various Camps, notably at Green Point near Cape Town, and I always had to come to the conclusion that nothing could have been better. Is it likely that, when such an amount of care was bestowed upon the men, the women and children should have been made the objects of special persecution? No impartial person could believe such a thing to have been possible, and I feel persuaded that if the people who in England contributed to make the position of the British Government more difficult than already it was, could have glanced at some Prisoners' Camps, for instance, they would very quickly have recognised that an unbalanced sentimentality had exaggerated facts, and even in some cases distorted them.

In Green Point the prisoners were housed in double-storied buildings which had balconies running round them. Here they used to spend many hours of the day, for not only could they see what was going on around the Camps but also have a good view of the sea and passing ships. Each room held six men, and there was besides a large mess-room downstairs in each building

Rations

which held about ninety people. Each Boer officer had a room for himself. When, later on, the number of prisoners of war was increased, tents had to be erected to accommodate them; but this could hardly be considered hardship in the climate which prevails at the Cape, and cannot be compared to what at the present moment the soldiers of the Allies are enduring in the trenches. The tents were put in a line of twenty each, and each score had a building attached for the men in that line to use as a dormitory if they chose. Excellent bathrooms and shower-baths were provided, together with a plentiful supply of water. The feeding of the prisoners of war was on a substantial scale, the daily rations per man including :

Bread	... ...	1¼ lb.	Wood (or) ...	2 lb.
Meat (fresh)	...	1 lb.	Coal and wood ...	1½ lb.
Sugar	... ...	8 oz.	Vegetables ...	½ lb.
Coal (or) ...	...	1 lb.	Jam ¼ lb., or 6 oz. of vegetables in lieu.	

Coffee, milk and other items were also in like generous apportionments.

The clothing issued to the prisoners, as asked for by them, to give the month of June, 1901, as an instance, was :

Boots	... ...	148 pairs	Shirts	251
Braces	... ...	59 pairs	Socks	222 pairs
Hats	... ...	164	Trousers ...	166
Jackets	... ...	188	Waistcoats ...	87

and other small sundries.

Cecil Rhodes

At Green Point Camp ample hospital accommodation was provided for the sick, and there was a medical staff thoroughly acquainted with the Dutch language and Boer habits. There was electric light in every ward, as well as all other comforts compatible with discipline.

In the first six months of 1901 only five men died in the Camps, the average daily strength of which was over 5,000 men. As for the sick, the average rarely surpassed 1 per cent., amongst which were included wounded men, the cripples, and the invalids left behind from the parties of war prisoners sent oversea to St. Helena or other places.

The hospital diet included, as a matter of course, many things not forming part of the ordinary rations, such as extra milk, meat extracts, and brandy. A suggestive fact in that respect was that though the medical officers in charge of the Camps often appealed to Boer sympathisers to send them eggs, milk and other comforts for the sick prisoners, they hardly ever met with response; and in the rare cases when it happened, it was mostly British officials or officers' wives who provided these luxuries.

The spiritual needs of the prisoners of war were looked after with consideration; there was a recreation room, and, during the time that a large number of very young Boers were in Camps, an excellent school, in which the headmaster and assistant teachers held teachers' certificates. Under the Orange River Colony this school was later transferred to the Prisoners of War Camp at

Conditions in Camp

Simonstown, and in both places it did a considerable amount of good. The younger Boers took very kindly and almost immediately to English games such as football, cricket, tennis and quoits, for which there was plenty of room, and the British authorities provided recreation huts, and goal posts and other implements. The Boers also amused themselves with amateur theatricals, club-swinging, and even formed a minstrel troup called the " Green Point Spreemos."

In the Camps there was a shop where the Boers could buy anything that they required in reason at prices regulated by the Military Commandant. Beyond this, relatives and friends were allowed to send them fruit or anything else, with the exception of firearms. In the Boer laagers were coffee shops run by speculative young Boers. The prisoners used to meet there in order to drink coffee, eat pancakes and talk to heart's content. This particular spot was generally called Pan Koek Straat, and the wildest rumours concerning the war seemed to originate in it.

Now as to the inner organisation of the Camps. The prisoners were allowed to choose a corporal from their midst and also to select a captain for each house. Over the whole Camp there reigned a Boer Commandant, assisted by a Court of " Heemraden" consisting of ex-landrosts and lawyers appointed by the prisoners of war themselves. Any act of insubordination or inattention to the regulations, sanitary or otherwise, was brought before this court and the guilty party tried and sentenced. When the latter refused to abide by the judgment of the Boer court he was brought before the Military Commandant, but for this there was very seldom need.

The prisoners of war had permission to correspond with their friends and relatives, and were allowed newspapers and books. The former, however, were rather too much censored, which fact constituted an annoyance which, with the exertion of a little tact, might easily have been avoided.

As will be seen from the details, the fate of the Boer prisoners of war was not such a bad one after all. Nor, either, was life in the Concentration Camps, and I have endeavoured to throw some new light on the subject to rebut the old false rumours which, lately, the German Government revived when taxed with harsh treatment of their own prisoners of war, so as to draw comparisons advantageously to themselves.

While adhering to my point, I quite realise that it would be foolish to assert that all the Concentration Camps were organised and administered on the model of the Green Point Camp, where its vicinity to Cape Town allowed the English authorities to control everything that was going on. In the interior of the country things could not be arranged upon such an excellent scale, but had there not existed such a state of irritation all over the whole of South Africa—an irritation for which the so-called English loyalists must also share the blame—matters would not have grown so sadly out of proportion to the truth, painful though the facts were in some cases.

This question of the Camps was admittedly a most difficult one. It was the result of a method of warfare which was imposed upon England by circumstances, but for which no individual Minister or General was solely responsible. The matter was brought about by successive steps that turned out to be necessary, though they were deplorable in every respect. Failing the capture of the Boer commandoes, which was well-nigh impossible, the British troops were driven to strip the country, and stripping the country meant depriving not only the fighting men but also the women and children of the means of subsistence. Concentration, therefore, followed inevitably, and England found itself burdened with the immense responsibility of feeding, housing and clothing some sixty thousand women and children.

In spite of the British officers in charge of the Concentration Camps struggling manfully with this crushing burden of anxiety, and doing all that lay within their power to alleviate the sufferings of this multitude, cruel and painful things happened. The food, which was sufficient and wholesome for soldiers, could not do for young people, and yet it was impossible to procure any other for them. If the opinion of the military had been allowed to be expressed openly, one would have found probably that they thought England ought never to have assumed this responsibility, but rather have chosen the lesser evil and left these people on their farms, running the risk of the Boers provisioning themselves therefrom. The risk would not, perhaps, have been so great as could have been supposed at first sight, but then this ought to have been done from the very beginning of the war, and the order to burn the Boer farms ought never to have been given. But once the Boer farms had been deprived of their military use to the enemy, these people could not be turned back to starve on the veldt; the British had to feed them or earn the reproach of having destroyed a nation by hunger. As things had developed it was impossible for Great Britain to have followed any other policy—adopted, perhaps, in a moment of rashness, but the consequences had to be accepted. It only remained to do the best toward mitigating as far as possible the sufferings of the mass of humanity gathered into the Camps, and this I must maintain that the English Government did better than could have been expected by any who knew South Africa and the immense difficulties which beset the British authorities.

It must not be forgotten that when the war began it was looked upon in the light of a simple military promenade; and, who knows, it might have been that had not the Boers been just as mistaken concerning the intentions of England in respect of them as England was in regard to the Boer military strength and power of resistance. One must take into account that for the few years preceding the war, and especially since the fatal Jameson Raid, the whole of the Dutch population of the Transvaal and of the Orange Free State, as well as that of Cape Colony, was persuaded that England had made up its mind to destroy it and to give up their country, as well as their persons, into the absolute power of the millionaires who ruled the Rand. On their side the millionaires openly declared that the mines were their personal property, and that England was going to war to give the Rand to them, and thereafter they were to rule this new possession without any interference from anyone in the world, not even that of England. Such a state of things was absolutely abnormal, and one can but wonder how ideas of the kind could have obtained credence. But, strange as it may seem, it is an indisputable fact that the opinion was prevalent all over South Africa that the Rand was to be annexed to the British Empire just in the same way as Rhodesia had been and under the same conditions. Everyone in South Africa knew that the so-called conquest of the domain of King Lobengula had been effected only because it had been supposed that it was as rich in gold and diamonds as the Transvaal.

When Rhodes had taken possession of the vast expanse of territory which was to receive his name, the fortune-seekers who had followed in his footsteps had high anticipations of speedy riches, and came in time to consider that they had a right to obtain that which they had come to look for. These victims of money-hunger made Rhodes personally responsible for the disappointments which their greed and unhealthy appetites encountered when at last they were forced to the conclusion that Rhodesia was a land barren of gold. In time, perhaps, and at enormous expense, it might be developed for the purpose of cattle breeding, but gold and diamonds either did not exist or could only be found in such small quantities that it was not worth while looking for them.

As a result of this realisation, Rhodes found himself confronted by all these followers, who loudly clamoured around him their indignation at having believed in his assertions. What wonder, therefore, that the thoughts of these people turned toward the possibility of diverting the treasures of the Transvaal into their own direction. Rhodes was brought into contact with the idea that it was necessary to subdue President Kruger. With a man of Rhodes' impulsive character to begin wishing for a thing was sufficient to make him resort to every means at his disposal to obtain it. The Boer War was the work of the Rhodesian party, and long before it broke out it was expected, spoken of, and considered not only by the Transvaal Government, but also by the Burghers, who, having many opportunities of visiting the Cape as well as Rhodesia, had there heard expression of the determination of the South African League, and of those who called themselves followers and partisans of Rhodes, to get hold of the Rand, at the head of which, as an inevitable necessity, should be the Colossus himself. No denial of these plans ever came from Rhodes. By his attitude, even when relations between London and Pretoria were excellent, he gave encouragement to the people who were making all kinds of speculations as to what should happen when the Transvaal became a Crown Colony.

The idea of a South African Federation had not at that time taken hold of public opinion, and, if Rhodes became its partisan later on, it was only after he had realised that the British Cabinet would never consent to put Johannesburg on the same footing as Bulawayo and Bechuanaland. Too large and important interests were at stake for Downing Street to look with favourable eyes on the Rand becoming only one vast commercial concern. A line had to be drawn, but, unfortunately, the precise demarcation was not conveyed energetically enough from London. On the other hand, Cecil Rhodes, as well as his friends and advisers, did not foresee that a war would not put them in power at the Transvaal, but would give that country to the Empire to rule, to use its riches and resources for the good of the community at large.

The saddest feature of the South African episode was its sordidness. This robbed it of every dignity and destroyed every sympathy of those who looked at it impartially or from another point of view than that of pounds, shillings and pence. England has been cruelly abused for its conduct in South Africa, and abused most unjustly. Had that feeling of trust in the justice and in the straightforwardness of Great Britain only existed in the Dark Continent, as it did in the other Colonies and elsewhere, it would have proved the best solution to

Cecil Rhodes

all the entangled questions which divided the Transvaal Republic from the Mother Country by reason of its manner of looking at the exploitation of the gold mines. On its side too, perhaps, England might have been brought to consider the Boers in a different light had she disbelieved a handful of people who had every interest in the world to mislead her and to keep her badly informed as to the truth of the situation.

When war broke out it was not easy for the Command to come at once to a sane appreciation of the situation, and, unfortunately for all the parties concerned, the unjust prejudices which existed in South Africa against Sir Alfred Milner had to a certain extent tinctured the minds of people at home, exercising no small influence on the men who ought to have helped the High Commissioner to carry through his plans for the settlement of the situation subsequently to the war. The old saying, "Calumniate, calumniate, something will always remain after it," was never truer than in the case of this eminent statesman.

It took some time for matters to be put on a sound footing, and before this actually occurred many mistakes had been made, neither easy to rectify nor possible to explain. Foremost among them was this question of the Concentration Camps. Not even the protestations of the women who subsequently went to the Cape and to the Transvaal to report officially on the question were considered sufficient to dissipate the prejudices which had arisen on this unfortunate question.

A Critic on the Report

The best reply that was made to Miss Hobhouse, and to the lack of prudence which spoiled her good intentions, was a letter which Mrs. Henry Fawcett addressed to the *Westminster Gazette*. In clear, lucid diction this letter re-established facts on their basis of reality, and explained with self-respect and self-control the inner details of a situation which the malcontents had not given themselves the trouble to examine.

"First," says this forceful document, "I would note Miss Hobhouse's frequent acknowledgments that the various authorities were doing their best to make the conditions of Camp life as little intolerable as possible. The opening sentence of her report is, 'January 22.—I had a splendid truck given me at Cape Town through the kind co-operation of Sir Alfred Milner—a large double-covered one, capable of holding twelve tons.' In other places she refers to the help given to her by various officials. The commandant at Aliwal North had ordered £150 worth of clothing, and had distributed it; she undertook to forward some of it. At Springfontein 'the commandant was a kind man, and willing to help both the people and me as far as possible.' Other similar quotations might be made. Miss Hobhouse acknowledges that the Government recognise that they are responsible for providing clothes, and she appears rather to deprecate the making and sending of further supplies from England. I will quote her exact words on this point. The italics are mine. 'The demand for clothing is so huge that it is hopeless to think that the private

181

charity of England and Colonial working parties com-
bined can effectually cope with it. *The Government
recognise that they must provide necessary clothes*, and
I think we all agree that, having brought these people
into this position, it is their duty to do so. *It is, of
course, a question for English folk to decide how long
they like to go on making and sending clothes.* There
is no doubt they are immensely appreciated; besides,
they are mostly made up, which the Government clothing won't be.' Miss Hobhouse says that many of the
women in the Camp at Aliwal North had brought their
sewing machines. If they were set to work to make
clothes it might serve a double purpose of giving them
occupation and the power of earning a little money, and
it would also ensure the clothes being made sufficiently
large. Miss Hobhouse says people in England have very
incorrect notions of the magnificent proportions of the
Boer women. Blouses which were sent from England
intended for women could only be worn by girls of twelve
and fourteen; they were much too small for the well-
developed Boer maiden, who is really a fine creature.
Could a woman's out-out size be procured? It must be
remembered that when Miss Hobhouse saw the Camps
for the first time it was in January, the hottest month
in the South African year; the difficulty of getting supplies along a single line of rail, often broken by the
enemy, was very great. The worst of the Camps she
saw was at Bloemfontein, and the worst features of this
worst Camp were:

The Report: Some of the Findings

" 1. Water supply was bad.

" 2. Fuel was very scarce.

" 8. Milk was very scarce.

" 4. Soap was not to be had.

" 5. Insufficient supply of trained nurses.

" 6. Insufficient supply of civilian doctors.

" 7. No ministers of religion.

" 8. No schools for children.

" 9. Exorbitant prices were demanded in the shops.

" 10. Parents had been separated from their children.

" Within the Report itself, either in footnotes or in the main body of the Report, Miss Hobhouse mentions that active steps had already been taken to remedy these evils. Tanks had been ordered to boil all the water. She left money to buy another, and supplied every family with a pan to hold boiled water. Soap was given out with the rations. 'Moreover, the Dutch are so very full of resources and so clever they can make their own soap with fat and soda.' The milk supply was augmented; during the drought fifty cows only yielded four buckets of milk daily. 'After the rains the milk supply was better.' An additional supply of nurses were on their way. 'The Sister had done splendid work in her domain battling against incessant difficulties. . . . and to crown the work she has had the task of training Boer girls to nurse under her guidance.'

" Ministers of religion are in residence, and schools under Mr. E. B. Sargant, the Educational Commissioner, are open for boys and girls. Children have been reunited to parents, except that some girls, through Miss Hobhouse's kind efforts, have been moved away from the Camps altogether into boarding schools. Even in this Bloemfontein Camp, notwithstanding all that Miss Hobhouse says of the absence of soap and the scarcity of water, she is able to write: ' All the tents I have been in are exquisitely neat and clean, except two, and they are ordinary.' Another important admission about this Camp is to be found in the last sentence of the account of Miss Hobhouse's second visit to Bloemfontein. She describes the iron huts which have been erected there at a cost of £2,500, and says: ' It is so strange to think that every tent contains a family, and every family is in trouble—loss behind, poverty in front, privation and death in the present—but they have agreed to be cheerful and make the best of it all.'

" There can be no doubt that the sweeping together of about 68,000 men, women and children into these Camps must have been attended by great suffering and misery, and if they are courageously borne it is greatly to the credit of the sufferers. The questions the public will ask, and will be justified in asking, are:

" 1. Was the creation of these Camps necessary from the military point of view?

" 2. Are our officials exerting themselves to make the conditions of the Camps as little oppressive as possible?

The Defence

"8. Ought the public at home to supplement the efforts of the officials, and supply additional comforts and luxuries?

"The reply to the first question can only be given by the military authorities, and they have answered it in the affirmative. Put briefly, their statement is that the farms on the veldt were being used by small commandoes of the enemy as storehouses for food, arms and ammunition; and, above all, they have been centres for supplying false information to our men about the movements of the enemy, and correct information to the enemy about the movements of the British. No one blames the Boer women on the farms for this; they have taken an active part on behalf of their own people in the war, and they glory in the fact. But no one can take part in war without sharing in its risks, and the formation of the Concentration Camps is part of the fortune of war. In this spirit 'they have agreed,' as Miss Hobhouse says, 'to be cheerful and make the best of it.'

"The second question—'Are our officials exerting themselves to make the Camps as little oppressive as possible?'—can also be answered in the affirmative, judging from the evidence supplied by Miss Hobhouse herself. This does not imply that at the date of Miss Hobhouse's visit, or at any time, there were not matters capable of improvement. But it is confessed even by hostile witnesses that the Government had a very difficult task, and that its officials were applying themselves to grapple with it with energy, kindness and goodwill. Miss Hobhouse complains again and again of the difficulty of procuring soap. May I quote, as throwing light upon the fact that the Boer women were no worse off than the English themselves, that Miss Brooke-Hunt, who was in Pretoria to organise soldiers' institutes a few months earlier than Miss Hobhouse was at Bloemfontein, says in her interesting book, 'A Woman's Memories of the War': 'Captain —— presented me with a piece of Sunlight soap, an act of generosity I did not fully appreciate till I found that soap could not be bought for love or money in the town.' A Boer woman of the working-class said to Miss Brooke-Hunt: 'You English are different from what I thought. They told us that if your soldiers got inside Pretoria they would rob us of everything, burn our houses, and treat us cruelly; but they have all been kind and respectable. It seems a pity we did not know this before.' Miss Hobhouse supplies some rather similar testimony. In her Report she says: 'The Mafeking Camp folk were very surprised to hear that English women cared a rap about them or their suffering. It has done them a lot of good to hear that real sympathy is felt for them at home, and I am so glad I fought my way here, if only for that reason.'

"In what particular way Miss Hobhouse had to fight her way to the Camps does not appear, for she acknowledges the kindness of Lord Kitchener and Lord Milner in enabling her to visit them; we must therefore suppose that they provided her with a pass. But the sentence just quoted is enough in itself to furnish the answer to the third question—'Is it right for the public at home to supplement by gifts of additional comforts and luxuries the efforts of our officials to make Camp life as little intolerable as possible?' All kinds of fables have been told to the Boer men and women of the brutality and ferocity of the British. Let them learn by practical experience, as many of them have learnt already, that the British soldier is gentle and generous, and that his women-folk at home are ready to do all in their power to alleviate the sufferings of the innocent victims of the war. I know it will be said, ' Let us attend to the suffering loyalists first.' It is a very proper sentiment, and if British generosity were limited to the gift of a certain definite amount in money or in kind, I would be the first to say, ' Charity begins at home, and our people must come first.' But British generosity is not of this strictly measured kind. By all means let us help the loyal sufferers by the war; but let us also help the women and children of those who have fought against us, not with any ulterior political motive, but simply because they have suffered and are bound to suffer much, and wounded hearts are soothed and healed by kindness.

" Mr. Rowntree has spoken quite publicly of the deep impression made on the Boer women by the kindness shown them by our men. One said she would be always glad to shake hands with a British soldier; it was because of the kindly devices they had invented to make over their own rations to the women and children during the long journey when all were suffering from severe privations. Another Boer girl, referring to an act of kindness shown her by a British officer, remarked quietly: 'When there is so much to make the heart ache it is well to remember deeds of kindness.' The more we multiply deeds of kindness between Boer and Briton in South Africa, the better for the future of the two races, who, we hope, will one day fuse into a united nation under the British flag.''

I hope the reader will forgive me for having quoted in such abundance from Mrs. Fawcett's letter, but it has seemed to me that this plain, unprejudiced and un-sophisticated report, on a subject which could not but have been viewed with deep sorrow by every enlightened person in England, goes far to remove the doubts that might still linger in the minds of certain people ignorant of the real conditions of existence in South Africa.

A point insufficiently realised in regard to South African affairs is the manner in which individuals com-paratively devoid of education, and with only a hazy notion of politics, contrived to be taken into serious consideration not only by those who visited South Africa, but by a certain section of English society at home, and also in a more restricted measure by people at the Cape and in the Transvaal who had risen. These people pro-fessed to understand local politics better than the British authorities, and expected the officials, as well as public opinion in Great Britain, to adopt their advice, and to recognise their right to bring forward claims which they were always eager to prosecute. Unfortunately they had friends everywhere, to whom they confided their regrets that the British Government understood so very little the necessities of the moment. As these malcontents were just back from the Rand, there were plenty of people in Cape Town, and especially in Port Elizabeth, Grahamstown, and other English cities in Cape Colony, ready to listen to them, and to be influenced by the energetic tone in which they declared that the Boers were being helped all along by Dutch Colonials who were doing their best to betray the British.

In reality, matters were absolutely different, and those who harmed England the most at that time were precisely the people who proclaimed that they, and they alone, were loyal to her, and knew what was necessary and essential to her interests and to her future at the Cape of Good Hope and the Rand. Foremost amongst them were the adherents of Rhodes, and this fact will always cling to his memory—most unfortunately and most unjustly, I hasten to say, because had he been left absolutely free to do what he liked, it is probable he would have been the first to get rid of these encumbrances, whose interferences could only sow animosity where kindness and good will ought to have been put forward. Cecil Rhodes wanted to have the last and definite word to say in the matter of a settlement of the South African difficulties, and as no one seemed willing to allow him to utter it, he thought that he would contrive to attain his wishes on the subject by seeming to support the exaggerations of his followers. Yet, at the same time, he had the leaders of the Dutch party approached with a view of inducing them to appeal to him to put himself at their head.

This double game, which while it lasted constituted one of the most curious episodes in a series of events of which every detail was interesting, I shall refer to later in more detail, but before doing so must touch upon another, and perhaps just as instructive, question—the so-called refugees, whose misfortunes and subsequent arrogance caused so many anxious hours to Sir Alfred Milner during his tenure of office at the Cape and later on in Pretoria.

CHAPTER XIV

IN FLIGHT FROM THE RAND

ONE of the greatest difficulties with which the Imperial Government found themselves confronted when relations between Great Britain and the Transvaal became strained was the influx of refugees who at the first hint of impending trouble left Johannesburg and the Rand, and flocked to Cape Town.

The greater number were aliens. From Russia in particular they had flocked to the Transvaal when they heard of its treasures. Adventurers from other parts of Europe, with a sprinkling of remittance men, also deserted Johannesburg. Only the few were real English residents who, from the time the Rand had begun to develop, had been living and toiling there in order to win sufficient for the maintenance of their families. All this mass of humanity, which passed unnoticed when scattered over wide areas in the vicinity of Pretoria or Johannesburg, had lived for many years in the expectation of the day when the power of the Transvaal Republic would be broken. They had discounted it perhaps more than they should have done had the dictates of prudence been allowed to take the lead against the wishes of their hearts.

When war became imminent the big mining houses considered it wiser to close their offices and mines, and for these unfortunate beings, deprived of their means of existence, the position became truly a lamentable one. They could not very well remain where they were, because the Burghers, who had never taken kindly to them, made no secret of their hostility, and gave them to understand very clearly that as soon as war had been declared they would simply turn them out without warning and confiscate their property. Prudence advised no delay, and the consequence was that, beginning with the month of August, and, indeed, the very first days which followed upon the failure of the Bloemfontein Conference, a stream of people from the Transvaal began migrating toward Cape Colony, which was supposed to be the place where their sufferings would find a measure of relief that they vainly imagined would prove adequate to their needs. At the Cape, strangely enough, no one had ever given a thought to the possibility of such a thing happening. In consequence, the public were surprised by this persisting stream of humanity which was being poured into the Colony; the authorities, too, began to feel a despair as to what could be done. It is no exaggeration to say that for months many hundreds of people arrived daily from the north, and that so long as communications were kept open they continued to do so.

At first the refugees inundated the lodging-houses in Cape Town, but these soon being full to overflowing, some other means had to be devised to house and feed them. Committees were formed, with whom the Government officials in the Colony worked with great zeal and considerable success toward alleviating the misery with which they found themselves confronted in such an unexpected manner. The Municipal Council, the various religious communities, the Medical men—one and all applied themselves to relief measures, even though they could not comprehend the reason of the blind rush to the Cape. Nor, in the main, could the refugees explain more lucidly than the one phrase which could be heard on all sides, no matter what might have been the social position: " We had to go away because we did not feel safe on the Rand." In many cases it would have been far nearer to the truth to say that they had to go because they could no longer lead the happy-go-lucky existence they had been used to.

The most to be pitied among these people were most certainly the Polish Jews, who originally had been expelled from Russia, and had come to seek their fortunes at Johannesburg. They had absolutely no one to whom they could apply, and, what was sadder still, no claim on anyone; on the English Government least of all. One could see them huddling together on the platform of Cape Town railway station, surrounded by bundles of rags which constituted the whole of their earthly belongings, not knowing at all what to do, or where to go to. Of course they were looked after, because English charity has never stopped before differences of race and creed, but still it was impossible to deny that their constantly increasing number added considerably to the difficulties of the situation.

Cecil Rhodes

A Jewish Committee headed by the Chief Rabbi of Cape Town, the Rev. Dr. Bender, worked indefatigably toward the relief of these unfortunate creatures, and did wonders. A considerable number were sent to Europe, but a good many elected to remain where they were, and had to be provided for in some way till work could be found for them, which would at least allow them to exist without being entirely dependent on public charity. Among the aliens who showed a desire to remain in South Africa were many in possession of resources of their own; but they carefully concealed the fact, as, upon whatever it amounted to, they counted to rebuild their fortunes when Britain became sole and absolute mistress on the Rand.

The most dangerous element in the situation was that group of easygoing loafers who lived on the fringe of finance and picked up a living by doing the odd things needed by the bigger speculators. When things began to be critical, these idlers were unable to make money without working, and while prating of their patriotism, made the British Government responsible for their present state of penury. These men had some kind of instruction, if not education, and pretended they understood all about politics, the government of nations, and last, but not least, the conduct of the war. Their free talk, inflamed with an enthusiasm got up for the occasion, gave to the stranger an entirely incorrect idea of the position, and was calculated to give rise to sharp and absolutely undeserved criticisms concerning the conduct of the administration at home, and of the authorities in

An Atmosphere of Lies

the Colony. They also fomented hatred and spite between the English and the Dutch.

The harm done by these people, at a moment when the efforts of the whole community ought to have been directed toward allaying race hatred, and smoothing down the differences which had arisen between the two white sections of the population, is almost impossible of realisation for one who was not in South Africa at the time, and who could not watch the slow and gradual growth of the atmosphere of lies and calumny which gradually divided like a crevasse the very people who, in unison, might have contributed more than anything else to bring the war to a close. One must not forget that among these refugees who poisoned the minds of their neighbours with foundationless tales of horror, there were people who one might have expected to display sound judgment in their appreciation of the situation, and whose relatively long sojourn in South Africa entitled them to be heard by those who found themselves for the first time in that country. They were mostly men who could talk well, even eloquently; and they discussed with such apparent knowledge all the circumstances which, according to them, had brought about the war, that it was next to impossible for the new-comers not to be impressed by their language—it seemed bubbling over with the most intense patriotism.

The observer must take into account that among these people there happened to be a good many who, as the war went on, enrolled themselves in the various Volunteer

Corps which were formed. These gave the benefit of their experience to the British officers, who relied on the knowledge and perception of their informants because of themselves, especially during the first months which followed upon their landing, they could not come to a clearly focused, impartial judgment of the difficulties with which they found their efforts confronted. One must also remember that these officers were mostly quite young men, full of enthusiasm, who flamed up whenever the word rebellion was mentioned in their presence, and who, having arrived in South Africa with the firm determination to win the war at all costs, must not be blamed if in some cases they allowed their minds to be poisoned by those who painted the plight of the country in such a lugubrious tint. If, therefore, acts of what appeared to be cruelty were committed by these officers, it would be very wrong to make them alone responsible, because they were mostly done out of a spirit of self-defence against an enemy whom they believed to be totally different from what he was in reality, and who if only he had not been exasperated, would have proved of better and healthier stuff than, superficially, his acts seemed to indicate.

There was still another class of refugee, composed of what I would call the rich elements of the Rand: the financiers, directors of companies; managers and engineers of the different concerns to which Kimberley and Johannesburg owed their celebrity. From the very first these rightly weighed up the situation, and had been determined to secure all the advantages which it held for

anyone who gave himself the trouble to examine it
rationally. They came to Cape Town under the pretence
of putting their families out of harm's way, but in reality
because they wanted to be able to watch the development
of the situation at its centre. They hired houses at
exorbitant prices in Cape Town itself, or the suburbs, and
lived the same kind of hospitable existence which had
been theirs in Johannesburg. Their intention was to be
at hand at the settlement, to put in their word when the
question of the different financial interests with which
they were connected would crop up—as it was bound
to do.

The well-to-do executive class forming the last group
had the greatest cause to feel alarmed at the consequences
which might follow upon the war. Although they hoped
that they would be able to maintain themselves on the
Rand in the same important positions which they had
occupied previous to the war, yet they had enough
common sense to understand that they would not be
allowed under a British administration the same free
hand that President Kruger had given, or which they had
been able to obtain from him by means of " refreshers "
administered in some shape or other. It is true that they
had always the alternative of retiring from South Africa
to Park Lane, whence they would be able to astonish
Society, but they preferred to wait, in case the crash were
still delayed for some little time.

The big houses, such as Wernher, Beit and Co.—
the head of which, at Johannesburg, was Mr. Fred

Cecil Rhodes

Eckstein, a man of decided ability, who perhaps was one of those in South Africa who had judged the situation with accuracy—would have preferred to see the crisis delayed. Mr. Eckstein and other leading people knew very well that sooner or later the Transvaal was bound to fall to England, and they would have felt quite content to wait quietly until this event had been accomplished as a matter of course, by the force of circumstances, without violence. President Kruger was such an old man that one could, in a certain sense, discuss the consequences which his demise was bound to bring to South Africa. There was no real necessity to hurry on events, nor would they have been hurried had it not been for the efforts of the Rhodesians, whose complaints had had more than anything else to do with the failure of the Bloemfontein Conference, and all that followed upon that regrettable incident. It was the Rhodesians, and not the big houses of the Rand, who were most eager for the war.

The exploitation of Rhodesia, the principal aim of which was the foundation of another Kimberley, had turned out to be a disappointment in that respect, and there remained nothing but making the best of it, particularly as countless companies had been formed all with a distinctly mineral character to their prospectuses. Now, if the Rand, with all its wealth and its still unexplored treasures, became an appanage of Kimberley, it would be relatively easy to effect an amalgamation between gold and diamond mines, which existed there,

The Wrong Equation

and the Rhodesian companies. Under these conditions it was but natural that despite an intelligent comprehension of the situation, Sir Alfred Milner was nevertheless unable to push forward his own plans in regard to the Transvaal and its aged President, Mr. Kruger.

The misfortune of the whole situation, as I have already pointed out, was that the men who had attempted to play a high game of politics, in reality understood very little about them, and that instead of thinking of the interests of the Empire to which they professed themselves to be so deeply attached, they thought in terms of their personal outlook. Rhodes alone of those not in official position saw the ultimate aim of all these entangled politics. But unfortunately, though he had the capacities and experience of a statesman, he was not a patient man; indeed, throughout his life he had acted like a big spoiled child, to whom must be given at once whatever he desires. Too often he acted in the present, marring the future by thinking only of the immediate success of his plans, and brutally starting to work, regardless of consequences and of his personal reputation. Though his soul was essentially that of a financier and he would ride rough-shod over those who conducted their business affairs by gentler methods, yet at the same time, by a kind of curious contrast, he was always ready, nay, eager, to come to the material help of his neighbour— maybe out of affection for him; maybe out of that special sort of contempt which makes one sometimes throw a bone to a starving dog one has never seen before. The

Cecil Rhodes

greatest misfortune in Rhodes' life was his faculty, too often applied upon occasions when it were best suppressed, of seeing the mean and sordid aspects of an action, and of imagining that every man could be bought, provided one knew the price. He was so entirely convinced of this latter fact that it always caused him a kind of impatience he did not even give himself the trouble to dissimulate, to find that he had been mistaken. This happened to him once or twice in the course of his career.

The English party in the Colony regretted until the end of Rhodes' life the strange aberration that allowed the Raid, and made him sacrifice his reputation for the sake of hastening an event which, without his interference, would almost surely soon have come to pass. The salient feature of the Raid was its terrible stupidity; in that respect it was worse than a crime, for crime is forgotten, but nothing can efface from the memory of the world or the condemnation of history a colossally stupid political blunder.

After the foolish attempt to seize hold of their country, the Boers distrusted British honour and British integrity; and doubting the word or promises of England, they made her responsible for this mistake of Cecil Rhodes. Rhodes, however, refused to recognise the sad fact. The big magnates of Johannesburg said that the wisest thing Rhodes could have done at this critical juncture would have been to go to Europe, there to remain until after the war, thus dissociating himself from the whole question of the settlement, instead of intriguing to be entrusted with it.

The fact of Cecil Rhodes' absence would have cleared the whole situation, relieved Sir Alfred Milner, and given to the Boers a kind of political and financial security that peace would not be subject to the ambitions and prejudices of their enemies, but concluded with a view to the general interests of the country.

CHAPTER XV

DEALING WITH THE REFUGEES

THE refugees were a continual worry and annoyance to the English community at the Cape. As time went on it became extremely difficult to conciliate the differing interests which divided them, and to prevent them from committing foolish or rash acts likely to compromise British prestige in Africa. The refugees were for the most boisterous people. They insisted upon being heard, and expected the whole world to agree with their conclusions, however unstable these might be. It was absolutely useless to talk reason to a refugee; he refused to listen to you, but considered that, as he had been—as he would put it—compelled to leave that modern paradise, the Rand, and to settle at Cape Town, it became the responsibility of the inhabitants of Cape Town to maintain him. Table Mountain echoed with the sounds of their vain talk. They considered that they were the only people who knew anything about what the English Government ought to do, and who criticised it the most, threatening at every moment that they would write to their influential friends—even the poorest and most obscure had " influential friends "—revealing the abominable way in which English interests were neglected in Cape Colony, where the Government, according to them, only helped the rebels, and considered their wants and requirements in preference to those of their own people.

At first, when they were not known as they deserved to be, some persons fresh from the Mother Country, to whom South African morals and intrigues were unknown, took to heart the position as well as the complaints of those refugees. Hearing them continually mention cases in which rebel Dutch had, in this way or that, shown their want of allegiance to the British Government, conclusions were jumped at that there must exist a reason for these recriminations and allegations, and that British officials were in reality too anxious to conciliate the anti-English elements in the Colony, to the detriment of the loyalists, whose feelings of patriotism they considered, as a matter of course, required no reward and scarcely any encouragement. These people, unequipped with the truth, took up with a warmth which it certainly did not deserve the cause of these loyalists, sought their advice, and formed a totally wrong and even absurd opinion both as to South African politics and the conduct of the representatives of the Queen in Cape Town.

All the misrepresentation and misunderstanding which took place increasingly, led to animosity on the part of the Dutch. Rightly or wrongly, it was taken as a matter of course that Rhodes favoured the idea of a total annihilation of the Cape Dutch. And as he was considered a kind of demigod by so many the idea was widely circulated, and became at last deeply rooted in the minds of most of the white population of South

Africa, who, without being able to say why, considered it in consequence a part of its duty to exaggerate in the direction of advocating severity toward the Dutch. This did not contribute to smoothen matters, and it grew into a very real danger, inimical to the conclusion of an honourable and permanent peace. Federation, which at one time had been ardently wished for almost everywhere, became a new cause for anxiety as soon as it was known that Rhodes was in favour of it. People fancied that his ambitions lay in the direction of a kind of dictatorship exercised by himself over the whole of South Africa, a dictatorship which would make him in effect master of the country.

This, however, was the last thing which the financiers on the Rand wished. Indeed, they became quite alarmed at the thought that it might become possible, and hastened to explain to Sir Alfred Milner the peril which such a thing, if it ever happened, would constitute for the community at large. Their constant attendance upon Sir Alfred, however, gave rise to the idea that these financiers wanted to have it all their own way with him and with the Cabinet at home, and that they meant to confiscate the Transvaal to their own profit.

The presence of the moneyed class at the Cape had also another drawback: it exasperated the poorer refugees, who could not forgive those who, too, had fled the Rand, for having so successfully saved their own belongings from the general ruin and remained rich, when so many of those who had directly or indirectly helped them to acquire their wealth were starving at their door. In reality the magnates of the Rand spent huge sums in the relief of their poorer brethren in misfortune. I know from personal experience, having often solicited them in favour of, say, some unfortunate Russian Jew or a destitute Englishman who had lost all his earthly belongings through the war. These millionaires, popularly accused of being so hardhearted, were always ready with their purses to help those who appealed to their charity. But the fact that they were able to live in large and luxurious houses whilst so many others were starving in hovels, that their wives wore diamonds and pearls, and that they seemed still to be able to gratify their every desire, exasperated the multitude of envious souls congregated at the Cape.

A general feeling of uneasiness and of unpleasantness began to weigh on the whole atmosphere, and as it was hardly possible for anyone to attack openly those who had inexhaustible purses, it became the fashion to say that the Dutch were responsible for the general misfortune, and to discover means of causing them unpleasantness.

On the other hand, as the war went on and showed no signs of subsiding, the resources of those who, with perfect confidence in its short duration, had left the Rand at a moment's notice, began to dwindle the more quickly insomuch as they had not properly economised in the beginning, when the general idea was prevalent that the English army would enter Pretoria for the

Christmas following upon the beginning of the war, and that an era of unlimited prosperity was about to dawn in the Transvaal. I do believe that among certain circles the idea was rooted that once President Kruger had been expelled from the Rand its mines would become a sort of public property accessible to the whole community at large, and controlled by all those who showed any inclination for doing so.

The mine owners themselves looked upon the situation from a totally different point of view. They had gathered far too much experience concerning the state of things in South Africa to nurse illusions as to the results of a war which was bound to put an end to the corruption of the Transvaal Republic. They would have preferred infinitely to let things remain in the condition into which they had drifted since the Raid, because they understood that a strong British Government would be interested in putting an end to the abuses which had transformed the Rand into an annexe of the Stock Exchange of almost every European capital. But, as the war had broken out, they preferred that it should end in the establishment of a regular administration which could neither be bought nor persuaded to serve interests in preference to the public. They did not relish the possible triumph of a single man, backed by a powerful financial company, with whom they had never lived upon particularly affectionate terms.

Rather than see South Africa continue under the influence which had hitherto held it in grip, the magnates

A Fictitious Agitation

preferred to associate themselves with Sir Alfred Milner to bring about as soon as possible a Federation of the different South African States, where there would be no place for the ambition of a single individual, and where the domination of one financial company would become an impossibility. These magnates were reasonable people after all, quite content, after they had taken the cream, to allow others to drink. The fever for gold had left them. The fact was that these people were not at all anxious to remain at Johannesburg; they preferred to gather dividends in London rather than to toil in South Africa; the merry, merry days of the Rand had come to an end.

Altogether, indeed, things were beginning to slow down at Johannesburg, in spite of the fictitious agitation by the Rhodesian party. The war had come as a relief to everybody, and afforded the magnates the opportunity which they had been longing for, to enforce order and economy upon a stringent scale in their mines and to begin modelling their concerns after a European fashion, closing the door upon adventurers and cutting off the "financial fringe." The times when new fields of exploitation were discovered every day were at an end; the treasures which the Transvaal contained in the way of precious metals and stones had all been located; and very few surprises could be expected in that direction. It was time for the pioneers to retire upon their laurels and to give to themselves, as well as to their fortunes, the sedate appearance which they required in order to be able to take a place amid the most elegant and exclusive society of Europe. Had Rhodes remained alive he would have proved the one great obstacle which the magnates of the Rand would have to take into consideration, the disturbing element in a situation that required calm and quiet.

If Cecil Rhodes had been allowed to decide alone as to the best course of action to pursue he also might have come to the same conclusion as these magnates. During those moments when he was alone with his own thoughts and impulses he would have realised his duty toward his country. He was conscious, if others were not, of how utterly he had lost ground in South Africa, and he understood that any settlement of the South African difficulties could only become permanent if his name were not associated with it. This, though undeniable, was a great misfortune, because Rhodes understood so perfectly the art of making the best of every situation, and using the resources to hand, that there is no doubt he would have brought forward a practical solution of the problems which had cropped up on every side. He might have proved of infinite use to Sir Alfred Milner by his thorough knowledge of the Dutch character and of the leaders of the Dutch party with whom he had worked. But Rhodes was not permitted to decide alone his line of conduct : there were his supporters to be consulted, his so-called friends to pacify, the English Jingoes to satisfy, and, most difficult of all, the Bond and Dutch party to please. Moreover, he had been indulging in various intrigues of his own, half of which had been conducted through others and half carried out alone, with what he believed was success. In reality they proved to be more of these disappointments he had courted with a carelessness which would have appeared almost incredible if one did not know Cecil Rhodes. The Rhodesians, who with intention had contrived to compromise him, never left him a moment to his own thoughts. Without the flatterers who surrounded him Rhodes would undoubtedly have risen to the height of the situation and frankly and disinterestedly put himself at the disposal of the High Commissioner. But they managed so to irritate him against the representative of the Queen, so to anger him against the Dutch party to which he had belonged formerly, and so to persuade him that everybody was jealous of his successes, his genius and his position in South Africa, that it became relatively easy with a man of Rhodes' character to make him smart under the sense of nonappreciation. Thus goaded, Rhodes acted often without premeditation.

In contrast to this impatience and the sense of unsatisfied vanity, the coolness and greatness of character of Sir Alfred Milner appeared in strong contrast, even though many friends of earlier days, such as W. T. Stead, had turned their backs upon Sir Alfred, accusing him of being the cause of all the misfortunes which fell upon South Africa. But those who thus condemned Sir Alfred did not understand the peculiar features of the situation. He was credited with inspiring all the harsh measures which were employed on occasion by others, measures which he had stridently disapproved. Rhodes, in his place, would have killed somebody or destroyed something; Sir Alfred went slowly on with his work, disdained praise as well as blame, and looked toward the future. I leave it to the reader to decide which of the two showed himself the better patriot.

The refugees did not take kindly to the High Commissioner. They had been full of illusions concerning the help they fondly imagined he would be glad to offer them, and when they discovered that, far from taking them to his bosom, he discouraged their intention of remaining in Cape Town until the end of the war, they grumbled and lied with freedom. Sir Alfred gave them very distinctly to understand that they had better not rely on the British Government to feed and clothe them. He said that they would be well advised to try to find some work which would allow them to keep themselves and their families. But especially he recommended them to go back to Europe, which, he gravely assured the refugees, was the best place for them and their talents. This did not please those refugees who posed as martyrs of their English patriotism and as victims of the hatred of Kruger and of the Dutch. They expected to be petted and flattered as those looked up to as the saviours of the Empire.

All the foregoing applies to the middle-class section of the refugees. The poorer ones grumbled also, but in a different manner, and their irritation was rather directed towards the military authorities. As for the millionaires, with a few exceptions they also did not care for the High Commissioner for reasons elaborated in earlier pages of this volume. They even considered that it would be prejudicial to their interests to allow Rhodes to be upon too intimate terms with Sir Alfred Milner, so they kept a faithful watch at Government House as well as at Groote Schuur, and in doing so added to the tension which, up to the last moment of Sir Alfred's tenure of office at Cape Town, existed between him and Cecil Rhodes. Too courteous to tell his redoubtable adversary that he had better mind his own business, convinced, on the other hand, of the latter's great capacities and great patriotism, Sir Alfred was constantly doing all that he could do in reason to pacify him. Cecil Rhodes used to make most bitter and untrue remarks as to the stupidity of the Imperial Government at home and the incapacity of the men in charge of its armies in South Africa. All this was repeated right and left with the usual exaggeration, and reached, as perhaps was intended, those whom it concerned. The result was that Rhodes found himself tabooed at Pretoria. This he said was due to the great fear which his influence over public opinion in South Africa inspired among those in command there.

The big trouble with Rhodes was that he would never own himself in the wrong. He quibbled, he hesitated, he postponed replies to questions submitted for his consideration. He wearied everybody around him with his constant prevarications in regard to facts he ought to have accepted without flinching if he wanted to regain some of his lost prestige. Unfortunately for himself and for the cause of peace in South Africa, Rhodes fancied himself immensely clever at "biding his time," as he used to say. He had ever lurking somewhere in his brain the conviction that one day the whole situation at Cape Town and Pretoria would become so entangled that they would have to send for him to beg him as a favour to step round and by his magic touch unravel all difficulties. His curious shyness, his ambition and his vanity battled with each other so long that those in authority at last came to the sad conclusion that it was far better to look elsewhere for support in their honest efforts at this important moment in the existence of the African Continent.

One last attempt was made. It was backed up by people in London, among others by Stead. Stead liked the Great Imperialist as well as one man can like another, and had a great and justified confidence in Rhodes' good heart as well as in that indefinable nobility which manifested itself at times in his strange, wayward nature. Moreover, being gifted with a keen sense of intuition, the famous journalist realised quite well the immense work that might have been done by England through Rhodes had the latter consented to sweep away those men around him who were self-interested.

But Rhodes preferred to maintain his waiting attitude, whilst trying at the same time to accumulate as many proofs as possible that people wanted him to assert himself at last. It was the fact that these proofs were denied to him at the very minute when he imagined he held them already in his hands which led to his suddenly turning once more against the persons he had been almost on the point of propitiating. It led him to begin the movement for the suspension of the Constitution in Cape Colony, out of which he expected so much and which he intended to use as his principal weapon against the enemies whom he suspected. That was the last great political venture in his life; it failed, but merciful Providence allowed him not to see the utter collapse of his latest house of cards.

CHAPTER XVI

UNDER MARTIAL LAW

IT may be useful, or at any rate of interest, before I
lay my pen aside, to refer to several things which,
at the time they occurred, caused torrents of ink to flow
both in England and in South Africa.

The most important, perhaps, was the application of
martial law in Cape Colony. I must repeat that I hold
no brief for England. My affection and admiration for
her does not go to the extent of remaining absolutely
blind to faults she has made in the past, and perhaps is
making in the present. I will not deny that martial law,
which, unfortunately, is a necessity in wartime, was
sometimes applied with severity in South Africa. But
the odium rests principally on the loyalists; their spite-
ful information in many cases induced British officers
to treat as rebels people who had never even dreamt of
rebellion.

It must not be forgotten that those to whom was
entrusted the application of martial law had perforce
to rely on local residents, whom they could not possibly
suspect of using these officers to satisfy private animosities of further private interests. These British officers
had never been used to see suspicion reign as master,
or to watch a perfectly conscious twisting of the truth

214

in order to condemn, or even destroy, innocent people. A young and probably inexperienced officer sent into a small place like Aliwal North or Uitenhage, for instance, found himself obliged to rely for information as to the loyalty of the inhabitants on some adventurer who, through capitalist influence, had obtained an executive post of some kind. How can one wonder, therefore, that many regrettable incidents occurred and were immediately made capital of by the Bond party further to embitter the feelings of the Dutch Colonists?

Many illegal acts were performed under martial law; of some a mention was made in the Cape Town Parliament; these, therefore, do not admit of doubt. For instance, as Mr. Neethling said in the Legislative Council, a man of seventy was sent down from Paarl to Beaufort West without being allowed to say good-bye to his wife, who was left behind without means of support. Their house was searched for papers, but without result, and the man—a member of the Afrikander Bond —was sent back, after eighteen months' deportation, without any charge having been made against him. He was an auctioneer and shipping agent, and during his absence his business was annexed by a rival. One British Colonial, who held office at Stellenbosch, said to one family, without even making an inquiry as to their conduct, " You are rebels and I will take your mules "— which was done. The mules were afterwards sold to the Commissariat Department by the man who had commandeered them. Is it a matter of astonishment, therefore, that many people felt sore and bitter at all that they had undergone and were going through?

The administration of martial law in the country districts was absolutely deplorable; but when one examines minutely the circumstances of the cases of injustice about which one could have no doubt, it always emerged that these never proceeded from British officers, who, on the contrary, wherever they found themselves in command, invariably acted with humanity. The great mistake of the military authorities was that they had far too much confidence in the Volunteer Corps and those members of it who were only anxious to make money out of existing circumstances. Unfortunately, certain officers in command of the different corps were extreme Jingoes, and this distorted their whole outlook. People said at the time of the war that some districts of Cape Colony had been turned into hells; some things, in truth, called for strong comment. No words could be energetic enough to describe the manner in which martial law had been administered—in the district of Graaf Reinet, for instance. The commandants—this justice must be rendered to them—generally meant well, but, unfortunately, they were assisted by men of less stable character as intelligence officers. These, in their turn, unwisely without due inquiry, engaged subordinates, upon whom they relied for their information. Graaf Reinet people had had to put up with something akin to the Spanish Inquisition. Men there were afraid to speak for fear of espionage, the most innocent remarks were distorted by spies recruited from an uncertain section of the community. A cattle inspector was deported without trial; in consequence, the Secretary for Agriculture decided not to employ him again; at Graaf Reinet a Colonial intelligence officer constantly declared in public that it was his intention to drive the people into rebellion; and so instances could be multiplied.

The rebellion was not due to martial law. In Graaf Reinet the prison was frequently so crowded, often by men who did not in the least know why, that no more sleeping accommodation could be found in it. People were in durance vile because they would not join the town guard or defence force. So overcrowded the prison became that many persons contracted disease during their incarceration.

For these sad occurrences the Cape Government was not initially to blame; more than once they had remonstrated with the local military authorities, but reports concerning their conduct were not allowed to reach the ears of Lord Roberts or of Lord Kitchener. Very often a Hottentot informed against respectable citizens to the intelligence officer, and by virtue of that they were imprisoned as long as the military authorities deemed fit. When released, a man would sometimes find that his house had been sacked and his most valuable property carried away. Persons were deported at an hour's notice without reasons being given, and thereafter scouts took possession of their farms and plundered and destroyed everything. Four wagon-loads of men, women and children were deported from their homes at Beaufort West. In vain did they ask what they had done. Everybody of the name of Van Zyl in the district of Graaf Reinet was deported! not a single person was left on their farms except those who had driven them out of them. And after these had done their work the victims were told, "Now you can return home." Some had to walk back many miles to their farms, to find only ruin left. Many white people were imprisoned on the mere evidence of coloured persons, the reputation for veracity of whom was well known all over South Africa, and whose evidence against a white man would never have been admitted in any court of law previous to the war.

In Uitenhage the same kind of thing occurred. It was sufficient for a Boer column to pass near the farm of an Afrikander for the latter to be taken to prison without the slightest investigation. No one knew where the fines paid went, and certainly a good many of those which were imposed by the commanders of the scouts and volunteer corps never reached the coffers of the Government.

At Cradock, Somerset East, Graaf Reinet and Middelburg people were compelled to eradicate prickly pears and do other hard labour simply because they had remained quietly at home, according to the proclamation issued by Sir Alfred Milner, and refused to join a volunteer corps of some sort or other. Many magistrates, acting on instructions, forced guiltless people to walk a four to six hours' drive under the pretence of subduing their spirits.

One case especially was of such a flagrant nature that it illustrates how far the malice of these so-called loyalists went and the harm which their conduct did to the British Government. The act which I am going to relate would never have been committed by any genuine English officer, no matter under what provocation. There is also a detail which must be noticed: by a strange coincidence all the victims of oppression were, with but few exceptions, men of means, whom, therefore, it was worth while to plunder. The story is that a certain Mr. Schoeman, a man of wealth and position residing on Vlakteplaats, a farm in the division of Oudtshoorn, received, on August 28th, 1901, a message through his son from the military scouts who were stationed at De Jaeger's farm in the neighbourhood, instructing him to hand over his horses to their care. No written order from the Commandant was exhibited to Mr. Schoeman, either at that time or on his request, nor was any evidence adduced at his trial later on to prove that such an order had really been given by an officer administering martial law in the district. Nevertheless, Mr. Schoeman obeyed the order, and on the same afternoon sent his horses, three in number, to De Jaeger. The scouts refused to take his horses, and told them to bring them on the following morning, Thursday, August 29th. This Schoeman did; on coming to the place with them he found that the scouts had left, and was obliged to take the animals again back to his farm. On the afternoon of that same day he received a message from the scouts, and in reply told them to come and see him. He had meanwhile, for safety's sake, sent two horses to be concealed away from his stable, and kept one, a stallion, at the homestead.

The next day, Friday, Boers appeared early in the afternoon. They took the stallion, and the following day they returned and asked where the other horses were. Mr. Schoeman declined to give any information, but they discovered and seized them. Immediately after the Boers had left, Mr. Schoeman dispatched one of his farm boys named Barry to De Jaeger, the nearest military post, to report the occurrence. The scouts had, however, disappeared, and he learned from De Jaeger that before leaving they had received a report of the presence of the Boers. On the return of Barry, Mr. Schoeman endeavoured to obtain another messenger. Owing to the state of the country, which was infested with the enemy, his efforts proved unavailing.

During the next week Mr. Schoeman, with a considerable number of his neighbours, was ordered to Oudtshoorn. On his arrival he was arrested, without any charge or warrant, and confined for some three months, bail being refused. No preliminary examination was held as provided in the instructions on martial law issued May 1st, 1901. On Sunday, December 1st, it was notified to Mr. Schoeman that he would be tried on the following day, and the charges were for the first time communicated to him. On December 2nd the court assembled and Mr. Schoeman was charged with three offences:

1. For not having handed his horses over to the proper military authorities, whereby they fell into the hands of the enemy.

2. For having been on friendly terms with the enemy.

3. For having failed to report the presence of the enemy.

He was found guilty on the first and last charges and not guilty on the second count, being sentenced to six months' hard labour and to pay a fine of £500, or to suffer a further term of twelve months' hard labour in lieu of the fine. The sentence was confirmed, the fine was paid by Mr. Schoeman, and he underwent the imprisonment for one month with hard labour and for five months without hard labour, which was remitted upon order from Lord Kitchener, who, without even being fully instructed as to the circumstances of the case, of his own accord lightened the terrible sentence passed upon Mr. Schoeman.

Later on Mr. Schoeman was cleared of the calumnies that had been the cause of his suffering. In this case, as in many others, the victim was the object of the private vengeance of a man who had had a grudge against him, and repaid it in that abominable manner.

One of the worst mistakes among the many committed during the South African War was to allow residents to be invested with what was nothing less than unlimited authority over their fellow-citizens. The British Government, which was made responsible for these acts, would never have given its sanction to any one of them; mostly, it was unaware of the original facts. The English military authorities dealt in absolute good faith, which makes the more shameful the conduct of those who wilfully led them into error. Their one fault was not to realise that certain individuals were not fit to administer martial law. In one particular district the man in authority seemed to have as the single aim of his life the punishment of anyone with Dutch sympathies or of Dutch blood. It was useless to appeal to him, because whenever a complaint was brought by an inhabitant of the district he simply refused to listen to it, and poured a torrent of abuse at the head of the bringer. One of his most notorious actions was the treatment which, by his orders, was inflicted on an old man who enjoyed the general esteem of both the English and the Dutch community, a former member of the House of Assembly. His house was searched, the floors were taken up, and the whole garden was dug out of recognition in a search for documents that might have proved that his son, or himself, or any other member of his family had been in correspondence with the two Republics. All this kind of thing was done on hearsay evidence, behind which lay personal motives.

Had the settlement of the country been left entirely

The Dop Tax

in the hands of Lord Kitchener, nothing approaching what I have related could have occurred. Unfortunately for all concerned, this was precisely the thing which the Rhodesian and other interests opposed. Much of the loyalty, about which such a fuss was made at the Cape, was loyalty to the sovereign in the pocket, and not loyalty to the Sovereign on the throne. This concern for wealth was seen in many aspects of life in South Africa, and occasionally invaded drastically the realm of social well-being. A case in point was the opposition by the financial interests to a tax on brandy. In South Africa drunkenness was one of the worst evils, especially among the coloured race, yet the restrictive influence of a tax was withheld. The underlying motive was nothing but the desire to avoid the tax on diamonds, which every reasonable person claimed and considered to be a source of revenue of which the Government had no right to deprive itself. While Rhodes lived the legislation introduced and maintained by his powerful personality revealed the policy of compromise which he always pursued. He was eminently practical and businesslike. He said to the members of the Bond, " Don't you tax diamonds and I won't tax dop," as the Cape brandy is called. The compact was made and kept in his lifetime.

When Rhodes was dead and a big democratic British element had come into the country after the war, those in power began wondering how it was that diamonds, which kept in luxury people who did not live in the country and consequently had no interest whatever in its prosperity, were not taxed. The Ministry presided over by Sir Gordon Sprigg shared this feeling, and in consequence found itself suddenly forsaken by its adherents of the day before, and the Rhodesian Press in full cry against the Government. Sir Gordon Sprigg was stigmatised as a tool of the Bond and as disloyal to the Empire after the fifty years he had worked for it, with rare disinterestedness and great integrity. Nevertheless, the Ministry declared that, as there existed an absolute necessity for finding new resources to liquidate the expenses contingent on the war, it would propose a tax on diamonds and another one on dop.

The exasperation of the Rhodesian party, which was thus roused, was the principal reason why the agitation for the suspension of the Constitution in Cape Colony was started and pursued so vigorously in spite of the small chance it had to succeed. His support of this agitation may be called the death-bed effort of Rhodes. When he was no longer alive to lend them his strong hand, the Rhodesian party was bound to disperse. They tried in vain to continue his policy, but all their efforts to do so failed, because there was nothing really tangible for them to work upon.

With Cecil Rhodes came to an end also what can be called the romantic period of the history of South Africa, that period during which fortunes were made and lost in a few days; when new lands were discovered and conquered with a facility and a recklessness that reminded one of the Middle Ages. The war established an

Photo: Elliott & Fry.

THE RT. HON. SIR JOHN GORDON SPRIGG

equilibrium which but for it would have taken years to be reached. It sealed the past and heralded the dawn of a new day when civilisation was to assert itself, to brush away many abuses, much cruelty and more injustice. The race hatred which the personality of Rhodes had done so much to keep alive, collapsed very quickly after his death, and as time went on the work done with such unselfishness and such quiet resolution by Sir Alfred Milner began to bear fruit. It came gradually to be understood that the future would justify his aims.

The war was one of those colossal crises which shake the foundations of a country and change the feelings of a whole generation of men and women in regard to each other. Whilst it lasted it roused the worst passions and showed up the worst aspects of the character of the people who played a part in it; but once it was over the false fabric upon which the animosities of the day before had been built fell. A serious and more enlightened appreciation of the events that had brought about the cataclysm which had cleared the air took the place of the furious outburst of hatred that had preceded it. People began to realise that it was not possible, on a continent where Europeans constituted but a small minority, that they could give the coloured races a terrible example of disunion and strife and still maintain dominance. Both the English and Dutch had at last recognised the necessity for working together at the great task of a Federation of the South African States, which would allow the whole of the vast Southern Continent to develop itself on a plane of higher progress under the protection of the British flag. This Union was conceived many, many years earlier by Cecil Rhodes. It was his great spirit that thought of making into one great nation the agglomeration of small nationalities, white and black, that lay over the veldt and impenetrable forests of South and Central Africa. For a long space of years Cecil Rhodes was South Africa.

So long as Rhodes lived it would have been impossible for South Africa to escape the influence of his brain, which was always plotting and planning for the future whilst forgetting more often than was healthy or wise the preoccupations of the present. After the Queen's flag had been hoisted at Pretoria, Cecil Rhodes alive would have proved an anomaly in South Africa. Cecil Rhodes dead would still retain his position as a dreamer and a thinker, a man who always pushed forward without heeding the obstacles, forgetful of aught else but the end he was pursuing, the country which he loved so well, and, what he cared for even more, his own ambition. Men like Rhodes—with all their mistakes to mar their dazzling successes—cannot be replaced; it is just as difficult to take up their work as it is to fill the gap caused by their disappearance.

CONCLUSION

I HAVE come to the end of what I intended at first to be a book of recollections but which has resolved itself into one of impressions. A more competent pen than mine will one day write the inner history of this South African War, which by an anomaly of destiny had quite different results from those expected. So many things have occurred since it happened that the whole sequence of events, including the war, is now looked upon by many people as a simple incident in a long story.

In reality the episode was something more than that. It was a manifestation of the great strength of the British Empire and of the wonderful spirit of vitality which has carried England triumphantly through crises that would have wrecked any other nation. The incidents which followed the war proved the generosity that lies at the bottom of the English character and the grandeur that comes out of it in those grave moments when the welfare of a nation appears to be at stake and its rulers are unable to apply to a succession of evils and dangers the right remedy to bring about peace and contentment. No other nations possess this remarkable and distinctive feature. England very wisely refused to notice the bitterness which still persisted in the early days after the conclusion of peace, and devoted her energies to the one immense and immediate work of Federation.

The colossal work of Union had been conceived in the shape which it was eventually to assume by Sir Alfred Milner, who, after having laid the foundations, was patriot enough to allow others to achieve its consummation, because he feared the unjust estimate of his character, disseminated by interested persons, might compromise the desired object and far-reaching possibilities of an enterprise which the most sanguine had never imagined could be accomplished within so short a space of time. He had toiled courageously toward the founding of a new State where the rights of every white as well as of every coloured man should be respected and taken into account, and where it would be impossible for a handful of rich men by the mere power of riches to control the lives and consciences of others.

The time of Sir Alfred Milner's administration was the transitory period between the primitive and the civilised that no nation escapes, and this period Sir Alfred used in working toward the establishment of a strong and wise government. Whether the one which started its course of existence on the day when the Federation of South Africa became an accomplished fact was strong and wise it is not for me to say. At least it was a patriotic government, one which worked sincerely at the abolition of the race hatred which the war had not entirely killed, and also one which recognised that after all it was the principle of Imperial government that alone could bring back prosperity and security to unfortunate and bleeding South Africa.

The war gave to the Empire the loyal support and co-operation of the Dutch population at the Cape and also in the Transvaal, and the fidelity with which General Botha fulfilled his duty toward the Mother Country in the difficult moments of 1914 proved the strong link forged in 1902 between the British Empire and South Africa. Now that years have passed it is possible to look with a less passionate eye upon the past and upon the men who took a leading part in the events which gave to the British Empire another fair dominion. They appear to us as they really were, and we can more justly accord them their proper valuation. The personality of Cecil Rhodes will always remain a great one; his merits and his defects will be reduced to their proper relative proportions, and the atmosphere of adulation or antagonism which, as the occasion suited, was poured upon him, be dissipated by time's clarifying influences. His real work consisted in the opening of new sources of wealth and new spheres of activity to a whole multitude of his fellow-countrymen, and of giving his native land an extension of its dominions in regions it had never penetrated before Cecil Rhodes' enterprising spirit of adventure and of conquest sent him into the wilderness of Africa to open a new and radiating centre of activity and development for his country. The conception of the Cape to Cairo Railway was one of those projects for which his country will ever remain grateful.

Cecil Rhodes

Yes! Rhodes was a great Englishman in spite of his faults, and perhaps on account of his faults. Beside the genius of a Darwin or of a Pasteur, the talent of a Shakespeare or of a Milton, the science of a Newton or of a Lister, his figure seems a small one indeed, and it is absurd to raise him to the same level as these truly wonderful men. The fact that the activity of Cecil Rhodes lay in quite a different direction does not, however, diminish the real importance of the work which he did, nor of the services which he rendered to his country. The mistake is to judge him as a universal genius. His genius had a particular bent; it was always directed toward one point and one only, that of material advantages to be acquired for the nation to which he belonged and of which he was so proud to be the son. Without him South Africa would possibly have been lost for the British Empire, which owes him most certainly a great debt in that respect.

The years which have gone by since his death have proved that in many things Rhodes had been absolutely mistaken. Always he was an attractive, and at times even a lovable, personality; a noble character marred by small acts, a generous man and an unscrupulous foe; violent in temper, unjust in his view of facts that displeased him, understanding chiefly his personal interests, true to those whom he considered his friends, but implacable toward the people whom he himself had wronged. He was a living enigma to which no one had ever found a solution; because he presented constantly new and

Cortez as Prototype

unexpected sides that appeared suddenly and shattered the conclusion to which one had previously arrived.

In Europe Rhodes would not only have been impossible, but he would never have found the opportunity to give full rein to his faculties of organisation and of conquest. He knew no obstacles and would admit none in his way ; he was of the type of Pizarro and of Fernando Cortez, with fewer prejudices, far more knowledge, and that clear sense of civilisation which only an Englishman born and bred amid the traditions of liberty can possess. But he was lacking in the fine political conception of government which Sir Alfred Milner possessed, and whilst refusing to admit the thought of compromise in matters where a little yielding to the wishes and desires of others might have secured him considerable advantage, he yet allowed himself to become entangled in intrigues which he denied as soon as he perceived that they could not be successful, but for which the world always condemned and never forgave, and even in some cases despised him.

Notwithstanding the great brilliance of his intelligence and the strength of his mind, Cecil Rhodes will always be found inferior to the present Viscount Milner as a statesman. Rhodes could not and would not wait. Milner spent his whole existence in waiting, and waited so successfully that he lived to see the realisation of the plans which he had made and which so many, even among his friends, had declared to be quite impossible for him to realise. Milner, about whose tact and mental greatness so many false notions existed in South Africa as well as elsewhere, had been the one man who had seen clearly the consequences of the war. As he told me one day when we were talking about the regrettable race-hatred which lent such animosity to the struggle : "It will cease sooner than one thinks."

The wise administrator, who had studied human nature so closely as he had done politics, had based his judgments on the knowledge which he had acquired of the spirit of colonisation which makes Great Britain so superior to any other nation in the world, and his belief that her marvellous spirit of adaptation was bound to make itself felt in South Africa as it had elsewhere. Sir Alfred Milner knew that as time went on the Afrikanders would realise that their erstwhile enemies had given them the position to which they had always aspired, a position which entitled them to take a place among the other great nations of the world. He knew, too, that their natural spirit of pride and of vanity would make them cherish the Empire that had allowed them to realise their ambitions of the past. Until the war they had been proud of their gold and of their diamonds; after the war they would be proud of their country. And by the consciousness which would gradually come to them of the advantages which their Federation under the British flag had brought to them they would become also ardent British patriots—blessing the day when, in a passing fit of insanity, goaded into it by people who had never seen clearly the situation, President Kruger had declared war on England.

INDEX

233

Index

Index

Index

PRINTED BY CASSELL & COMPANY, LIMITED, LA BELLE SAUVAGE, LONDON, E.C.4
F 20.218

MX 000 432 846

Lightning Source UK Ltd.
Milton Keynes UK
UKOW06f0332230913

217643UK00003B/31/P